CASEBOOK SERIES

JANE AUSTEN: *'Northanger Abbey'* & *'Persuasion'* B.C. Southam
JANE AUSTEN: *'Sense and Sensibility'*, *'Pride and Prejudice'* & *'Mansfield Park'*
  B. C. Southam
BECKETT: *Waiting for Godot* Ruby Cohn
WILLIAM BLAKE: *Songs of Innocence and Experience* Margaret Bottrall
CHARLOTTE BRONTE: *'Jane Eyre'* & *'Villette'* Miriam Allott
EMILY BRONTE: *Wuthering Heights* (Revised) Miriam Allott
BROWNING: *'Men and Women'* & *Other Poems* J. R. Watson
CHAUCER: *The Canterbury Tales* J. J. Anderson
COLERIDGE: *'The Ancient Mariner'* & *Other Poems* Alun R. Jones & W. Tydeman
CONRAD: *'Heart of Darkness'*, *'Nostromo'* & *'Under Western Eyes'* C. B. Cox
DICKENS: *Bleak House* A. E. Dyson
DICKENS: *'Hard Times'*, *'Great Expectations'* & *'Our Mutual Friend''* Norman Page
DONNE: *Songs and Sonnets* Julian Lovelock
GEORGE ELIOT: *Middlemarch* Patrick Swinden
T.S. ELIOT: *Four Quartets*
T.S. ELIOT: *'Prufrock'*, *'Gerontion'* & *'Ash Wednesday'* B. C. Southam
T.S. ELIOT: *The Waste Land* C. B. Cox & Arnold P. Hinchliffe
HENRY FIELDING: *Tom Jones* Neil Compton
E.M. FORSTER: *A Passage to India* Malcolm Bradbury
HARDY: *The Tragic Novels* (Revised) R. P. Draper
HARDY: *Poems* James Gibson & Trevor Johnson
GERARD MANLEY HOPKINS: *Poems* Margaret Bottrall
HENRY JAMES: *'Washington Square'* & *'The Portrait of a Lady'* Alan Shelton
JONSON: *Volpone* Jonas A. Barish
JAMES JOYCE: *'Dubliners'* & *'A Portrait of the Artist as a Young Man'* Morris Beja
KEATS: *Odes* G. S. Fraser
KEATS: *Narrative Poems* John Spencer Hill
D.H. LAWRENCE: *Sons and Lovers* Gamini Salgado
D.H. LAWRENCE: *'The Rainbow'* & *'Women in Love'* Colin Clarke
LOWRY: *Under the Volcano* Gordon Bowker
MARLOWE: *Doctor Faustus* John Jump
MARLOWE: *'Tamburlaine the Great'*, *'Edward II'* & *'The Jew of Malta'* J. R. Brown
MILTON: *Paradise Lost* A.E. Dyson & Julian Lovelock
O'CASEY: *'Juno and the Paycock'*, *'The Plough and the Stars'* & *'The Shadow of a
  Gunman'* Ronald Ayling
JOHN OSBORNE: *Look Back in Anger* John Russell Taylor
PINTER: *'The Birthday Party'* & *Other Plays* Michael Scott
POPE: *The Rape of the Lock* John Dixon Hunt
SHAKESPEARE: *A Midsummer Night's Dream* Antony Price
SHAKESPEARE: *Antony and Cleopatra* (Revised) John Russell Brown
SHAKESPEARE: *Coriolanus* B. A. Brockman

The Metaphysical Poets

A CASEBOOK

EDITED BY

GERALD HAMMOND

First published 1974 by
THE MACMILLAN PRESS LTD
Houndmills, Basingstoke, Hampshire RG21 2XS
and London
Companies and representatives
throughout the world

ISBN 0–333–15466–5

Printed and bound in Great Britain by
Antony Rowe Ltd, Chippenham and Eastbourne

TO PATSY

CONTENTS

ACKNOWLEDGEMENTS

S. L. Bethell, 'The Nature of Metaphysical Wit', from *Northern Miscellany of Literary Criticism*, 1 (1953) by permission of Mrs M. R. Bethell; Rosalie L. Colie, from 'Style and Stylistics', in *'My Ecchoing Song'* : *Andrew Marvell's Poetry of Criticism*, © 1970 by Princeton University Press, pp. 75–96, reprinted by permission of Princeton University Press; T. S. Eliot, 'The Metaphysical Poets', from *Selected Essays*, reprinted by permission of Faber & Faber Ltd and Harcourt Brace Jovanovich Inc., new edition by T. S. Eliot, © 1932, 1936, 1950, by Harcourt Brace Jovanovich Inc., © 1960, 1964, by T. S. Eliot; Josephine Miles and Hanan C. Selvin, 'A Factor Analysis of the Vocabulary of Poetry in the Seventeenth Century', from *The Computer and Literary Style*, ed. Jacob Leed (1966), by permission of The Kent State University Press; Earl Miner, 'Alteration of Time', from *The Metaphysical Mode from Donne to Cowley*, © 1969 by Princeton University Press, pp. 99–117, reprinted by permission of Princeton University Press; Leo Spitzer, from 'Three Poems on Ecstasy', in *Essays on English and American Literature by Leo Spitzer*, ed. Anna Hatcher, © 1962 by Princeton University Press, pp. 142–53, reprinted by permission of Princeton University Press; Joseph H. Summers, 'The Conception of Form', from *George Herbert: His Religion and His Art,* by permission of Chatto & Windus Ltd and Harvard University Press 1954; Rosemond Tuve, from *Elizabethan Metaphysical Imagery* (1947), by permission of The University of Chicago Press.

GENERAL EDITOR'S PREFACE

Each of this series of Casebooks concerns either one well-known and influential work of literature or two or three closely linked works. The main section consists of critical readings, mostly modern, brought together from journals and books. A selection of reviews and comments by the author's contemporaries is also included, and sometimes comments from the author himself. The Editor's Introduction charts the reputation of the work from its first appearance until the present time.

The critical forum is a place of vigorous conflict and disagreement, but there is nothing in this to cause dismay. What is attested is the complexity of human experience and the richness of literature, not any chaos or relativity of taste. A critic is better seen, no doubt, as an explorer than as an 'authority', but explorers ought to be, and usually are, well equipped. The effect of good criticism is to convince us of what C. S. Lewis called 'the enormous extension of our being which we owe to authors'. A Casebook will be justified if it helps to promote the same end.

A single volume can represent no more than a small selection of critical opinions. Some critics have been excluded for reasons of space, and it is hoped that readers will follow up the further suggestions in the Select Bibliography. Other contributions have been severed from their original context, to which some readers may wish to return. Indeed, if they take a hint from the critics represented here, they certainly will.

A. E. DYSON

INTRODUCTION

I

It would, therefore, seem in the interest of precise communication to avoid the word 'metaphysical' whenever possible. The following words, among others, convey most of the meanings intended by the term in the past: 'great', 'passionate', 'disillusioned', 'sceptical', 'intellectual', 'rational', 'philosophical', 'theological', 'sensual', sensuous', 'conversational', 'anti-poetic', and 'rough'. Perhaps most useful, since it is so awkward it would not be abused, is 'Donne-like'.

These words, from a note in Joseph Summers's book on George Herbert, express very clearly the irritation felt by critics at the use of the word 'metaphysical' to describe a number of seventeenth-century English poets. Since De Quincey it has become a critical reflex action to deprecate the word as vague and misleading, and to suggest an alternative. Unfortunately there has not been any consensus as to what that alternative should be.

The responsibility for the currency of the word 'metaphysical' is Dr Johnson's. Previous to his 'Life of Cowley' (1779) there was no such person as a metaphysical poet, and no such race as the metaphysical poets. 'Metaphysical' had been a term applied to witty, conceited poetry, but in the vaguest possible way. The earliest uses of the word, by the Italian poet Testi (1593–1646) – 'concetti metafisici et ideali' – and by Drummond of Hawthornden (1585–1649) – 'Metaphysical *Ideas* and Scholastical *Quiddities*' – were derogatory. Applied to a particular poet, John Cleveland, the word carried a similar sneer:

> Call *him* th' *Muses Metaphysick Reader;*
> Of all the Poets *Troup* stile him the *Leader;*
> Who with rare Novelties baffles the Sense
> Of the busie pated *Weeks* intelligence,
>
> (Austin, *Naps Upon Parnassus,* 1658)

Cleveland himself used the words to convey affection, in his poem
'The Hetacomb to his Mistress' :

> Call her the Metaphysics of her sex,
> And say she tortures wits as quartans vex
> Physicians . . .

Towards the end of the century, in a fawning dedication to
Dorset, Dryden made the oft-quoted remark that Donne 'affects
the metaphysics, not only in his satires, but in his amorous verses,
where nature only should reign'. After Dryden 'metaphysical'
came to be used more often in reference to Donne and his
followers (as in the extracts on pp. 47 and 49). Its most notable use was by Pope, reported in Spence's *Anecdotes,* who
referred to the 'metaphysical style' which Cowley had borrowed
from Donne (and Johnson may well have seen the *Anecdotes*
in manuscript before writing his *Lives of the Poets*). But before
Johnson 'metaphysical' had not become the label it is today.
Pope, in his table of English poets given in Ruffhead's *Life,*
catalogued a 'School of Donne'. Addison used the phrase 'mixt
wit'. Gray's classification of English poets included 'a third
Italian school, full of conceit'. Theobald's preface to his edition
of Shakespeare talked of Shakespeare's contemporaries in the following way : '. . . a wonderful Affectation to appear Learned . . .
the forced, quaint, unnatural Tract they were in . . . The
ostentatious Affectation of abstruse Learning . . . this Habit of
Obscurity.' 'Metaphysical', as a term of description or disap-
probation, was resolutely ignored.

After Johnson's 'Life of Cowley' 'metaphysical' began its growth into the vague, misleading term it is today. At first it was applied only to those poets Johnson had mentioned – Donne, Cowley and Cleveland – but its use gradually widened over the next two centuries to include all the followers of Donne, the exponents of strong lines, the baroque poets. That process of expansion is the theme of this Introduction.

II

Johnson's 'Life of Cowley' did more than establish the term 'metaphysical poets'; it contained the first detailed and discriminating discussion of their works. Donne's reputation had survived into the eighteenth century largely for his wit and learning. As a poet he was disparaged, either indirectly, as in Pope's 'versifying' of his satires, or openly, as in the 'Poetical Scale' given in the *Literary Magazine* in 1758. The scale gave a possible eighty points to poets for 'Genius, Judgment, Learning, Versification'. Pope came top with 80 points, then came Milton and Dryden with 69, Addison with 68, Shakespeare and Cowley with 66 and Spenser with 62. Donne was omitted from the scale because, although a man of wit, 'he seems to have been at pains not to pass for a poet'. Between 1719 and 1779 no editions of Donne appeared, so that for many readers the quotations in Johnson's 'Life' were their first opportunity to read Donne's poetry.

As the *Literary Magazine*'s scale implies, Abraham Cowley was the best known of the metaphysical poets in the eighteenth century. Three editions of his works appeared in the first quarter of the century, but, because of his metaphysical qualities, he came to be seen more and more as a primitive. James Granger's *Biographical History of England* (1769) cast him as one 'who helped to corrupt the taste of the age in which he lived, and had himself been corrupted by it'. Collected works of Cowley gave way to selected works, and the literary theorists, such as Lord Kames and Hugh Blair, used his poems as stock examples of bad taste and vicious judgement. William Cowper's tone is nostalgic for an adolescent taste he had outgrown :

> Thee too, enamour'd of the life I lov'd,
> Pathetic in its praise, in its pursuit
> Determin'd and possessing it at last
> With transports such as favour'd lovers feel,
> I studied, priz'd and wish'd that I had known
> Ingenious Cowley! and, though now reclaim'd
> By modern lights from an erroneous taste,
> I cannot but lament thy splendid wit
> Entangled in the cobwebs of the schools.
>
> <div align="right">(<i>The Task</i>, IV, 718–26)</div>

The other metaphysical poets well known in the eighteenth century were Francis Quarles and George Herbert. Like Cowley, both were read for reasons other than their metaphysical qualities. Quarles, throughout the century, was the butt of the *literati*, from Pope's *Dunciad* to James Beattie's crushing dismissal in his *Essays* (1776): 'Examples of bad writing might no doubt be produced on almost any occasion, from Quarles and Blackmore, but as no body reads their works, no body is liable to be misled by them ....'

But Beattie was wrong. Quarles's *Emblemes* was reprinted regularly in the eighteenth century, and there are many other indications that he continued to be, as Edward Phillips had described him in 1675, 'the darling of our plebian judgements'. Clearly the manifest piety of the *Emblemes* attracted a great lower middle-class readership, hence the proliferation of such editions as *Francis Quarles' Emblems and Hieroglyphicks of the Life of Man Modernised* (1773?). The moderniser felt that Quarles's poetry had something important to say. He gave reasons for modernising which explain why eighteenth-century readers found metaphysical poetry so rough and graceless:

Many of his Phrases are so affected that no Person who had any Taste for Reading can peruse them with the least Degree of Pleasure. Many of his Expressions are harsh, and sometimes whole Lines are included within a Parenthesis, by which the Mind of the Reader is diverted from the Principal Object.

George Herbert also found his main eighteenth-century readership in a group separate from the *literati*. His volume of verse, *The Temple*, published a few months after his death in 1633, had exerted tremendous influence upon the mid-seventeenth-century poets. Henry Vaughan in his own preface to his volume of sacred verse, *Silex Scintillans* (1654), spoke of 'Mr. George Herbert, whose holy *life* and *verse* gained many pious converts (of whom I am the least) and gave the first check to a most flourishing and admired *wit* of his time'. Vaughan's debt to Herbert is obvious. His verse is full of echoes of Herbert's poetry, and his volume has the same sub-title as *The Temple*, 'Sacred Poems and Private Ejaculations'. Richard Crashaw called his first volume of sacred poetry *Steps to the Temple* (1646); the anonymous preface used Herbert's name to emphasise Crashaw's claim to fame. 'Here's *Herbert's* second, but equall, who hath retriv'd Poetry of late, and return'd it up to its Primitive use....'

The most amusing evidence of Herbert's influence is Christopher Harvey's volume *The Synagogue: Or the Shadow of the Temple* (1640), which was bound in with Herbert's *Temple* for the next two hundred years on the basis that the reader who liked Herbert's poetry would inevitably like Harvey's. The opening poem of *The Synagogue*, 'A Stepping Stone to the Threshold of Mr. Herbert's Church Porch', demonstrates both Harvey's ability and the awe he felt for Herbert:

> In Building of his Temple, Master *Herbert*
> Is Equally all Grace, all Wit, all Art.
> *Roman* and *Grecian* Muses all give way :
> One *English* Poem darkens all your day.

The whole volume reads like a bizarre anthology of Herbertisms, in syntax, form and diction. 'Church Festivals', for instance, combines the parataxis of such Herbert poems as 'Prayer (I)' with ponderous attempts at wit. The result is chaos :

> Marrow of time, Eternity in brief,
> Compendiums Epitomiz'd, the chief
> Contents, the Indices, the Title-pages
> Of all past, present, and succeeding ages,
> Sublimate graces, antidated glories,
> The cream of holiness,
> The inventories
> Of future blessedness
> The florilegia of celestial stories . . .

As the taste for metaphysical poetry declined, Herbert's reputation as a pious man took over, based firmly on Izaak Walton's *Life* (1670). His poetry became recommended reading for children for instruction in piety and, like Quarles, he retained a large middle-class readership more interested in the message than the poetry. *The Temple* was reprinted three times in the first eleven years of the eighteenth century, and then not again until 1799. But at least sixteen collections of verse in the period 1695–1790 contained poems by Herbert. The most important of these was John Wesley's *Hymns and Sacred Poems* (1739), which included over forty poems from *The Temple*. In many cases these poems were heavily rewritten.

Often the eighteenth-century's rewriting of earlier verse made graceful and calm what was originally rough and forceful, as in these two openings to versions of Donne's 'The Canonization' in the *Gentleman's Magazine* in 1761 :

(i) Forbear thy grave advice, and let me love,
    Or lay on nature, not on me, the blame :
    Can words the venerable snow remove
    From age's head, or quench a fever's flame?
    As soon the winged hours at thy request
    May cease to fly, as love forsake my breast . . .

(ii) I prithee cease to chide my guiltless love,
    Nor tire my patience with thy loath'd advice
    Can'st thou expect a soul like mine to move,
    Or tempt my youth to sordid avarice?
    In vain; the selfish arts of heaping gold
    As ill become the young as love the old . . .

Herbert's poem 'Vertue' was rewritten at least three times. One
version, in the *Universal Magazine* in 1788, kept the short last
line of each stanza, but transformed Herbert's celebration of the
invincibility of virtue into a *carpe diem* plea :

> Sweet Day ! so bland, so fair, so bright
>   The garnisher of earth and sky;
> Soft dews shall weep thy fall to night,
>   For thou must die.
>
> Sweet Spring ! full of sweet days and pleasures.
>   In Expectation's youthful eye,
> Thy fragrant airs and melting measures
>   Alike must die.
>
> Sweet Rose, whose bloom such hues discover,
>   As quick vermilion comes not nigh;
> Thy root e'en now the grave doth cover
>   Where thou may'st die.
>
> Then since each good that time supposes
>   From changeful seasons feels decay;
> From pleasure cull perennial posies :
>   Live while you may.

Another version, in *The Charmer* in 1765, made the stanzas regular, and turned the poem into a praise of wedded love :

> Sweet day, so cool, so calm, so bright
> The bridal of the earth and sky,
> The dew shall weep thy fall tonight,
> For thou, with all thy sweets, must die.
>
> Sweet rose, so fragrant and so brave,
> Dazzling the rash beholder's eye,
> Thy root is ever in its grave,
> And thou, with all thy sweets, must die.
>
> Sweet spring, full of sweet days and roses,
> A box, where sweets compacted lie,
> Not long ere all thy fragrant posies,
> With all their sweets, must fade and die.
>
> Sweet love alone, sweet wedded love,
> To thee no period is assign'd;
> Thy tender joys by time improve,
> In death itself the most refin'd.

Wesley's rewritting of 'Vertue' came closer than these two to the sentiment of the original, but rigorously ironed out most of the conceits and turns of wit :

> Sweet Day, so cool, so calm, so bright,
> The Bridal of the Earth and Sky :
> The Dew shall weep thy Fall to-night
> For thou with all thy Sweets must die !
>
> Sweet Rose, so fragrant and so brave,
> Dazzling the rash Beholder's Eye :
> Thy Root is ever in its Grave,
> And thou with all thy Sweets must die !

> Sweet Spring, so beauteous and so gay,
>   Storehouse where Sweets unnumber'd lie :
> Not long thy fading Glories stay,
>   But thou with all thy Sweets must die !
>
> Only a sweet and virtuous Mind,
>   When Nature all in Ruins lies,
> When Earth and Heaven a Period find,
>   Begins a Life that never dies !

Eighteenth-century attitudes to other metaphysical poets are not illuminating. Cleveland became an object of scorn. Vaughan was unknown. Marvell's statesmanship was extolled, his poetry forgotten. An attempt to revive Crashaw's reputation was made by one Peregrine Philips in 1785, but his selection, *Poetry by Richard Crashaw*, aroused widespread hostility because of his accusations of plagiarism against a number of English poets, including Gray, Pope and Milton.

Johnson's dissertation on metaphysical poets in the 'Life of Cowley' seems, at first glance, to have done little to counteract the age's ignorance. The illustrative quotations were limited to three poets, Cowley, Donne and Cleveland, and there was no mention of such major figures as Herbert, Vaughan, Marvell or Crashaw. But a closer reading of the dissertation reveals a strong underlying sense of there being a whole host of lesser metaphysical lights. Running through it is a constant refrain of '. . . race of writers . . . this race of authors . . . this species of poets . . . the authors of this race . . . these writers . . . almost the last of that race . . .'. If Boswell's response is typical, the reading public's appetite was keenly whetted :

The Life of Cowley he himself considered the best of the whole, on account of the dissertation which it contains on the *Metaphysical Poets*. . . . Johnson has exhibited them at large, with such happy illustrations from their writings, and in so luminous a manner, that

indeed he may be allowed the full merit of novelty, and to have
discovered to us, as it were, a new planet in the poetical atmosphere.

III

The 'Life of Cowley' was a catalyst. It stimulated readers to go
back to the metaphysical poets, and the years between it and
Victoria's accession show a growing knowledge of the works of
Donne, Herbert, Vaughan, Quarles, Crashaw and Marvell.
References to these poets by reviewers assumed a familiarity with
them on the part of the general reading public. The *Critical
Review* in 1791 warned modern poets of the danger of alienat-
ing readers by pursuing obscurity for obscurity's sake, i.e. 'the
same error with Cowley, and the rest of those abstract metaphysical poets . . . [whose] works constitute a sort of perpetual
puzzle or enigma'. The *Edinburgh Review* in 1802 wrote of a
modern sect of poets, one of whose sources was 'the quaintness
of Quarles and Dr. Donne'. The *Eclectic Review* in 1816 found
in Wordsworth 'the singular combination of the metaphysical
poet, the enthusiastic lover, and minute observer of external
nature'.

The reviewers were right in so far as the Romantics did
respond enthusiastically to the newly discovered poetry. Donne
was praised in turn by Lamb, Coleridge and De Quincey.
Crashaw's poetry was familiar to Shelley, and influenced Coleridge's 'Christabel'. General response to the metaphysicals was
stimulated by the appearance of new and attractive editions.
Herbert's *Temple*, for example, was reprinted in 1799, 1805 and
1809; and Coleridge's notes on the verse indicate the beginnings
of a critical rather than pietistic response. During this period
Vaughan's poetry emerged from oblivion. First came three
stanzas in an 1801 collection of early English poetry; then he was

honoured with a derogatory mention by Thomas Campbell in his *Specimens of the British Poets* in 1819: 'He is one of the harshest even of the inferior order of the school of conceit; but he has some few scattered thoughts that meet our eye amidst his harsh pages like wild flowers on a barren heath.' That opinion did not prevent Campbell from borrowing a few of Vaughan's lines to adorn his own verse, a piece of plagiarism exposed in *Blackwood's Magazine* in 1825.

The first edition of Vaughan's verse since the seventeenth century appeared in 1847, edited by the Reverend H. F. Lyte. Significantly Lyte echoed the judgement of another reverend gentleman, Robert Willmott, who had answered Campbell's criticism by finding in Vaughan's sacred poems 'considerable originality and picturesque grace'. In fact the first serious critical reading of Vaughan, in the *Retrospective Review* in 1820, had been devoted to his volume of secular poetry, *Olor Iscanus*. The reviewer opened his article by deploring the fact that Vaughan had been ignored for so long. He could not, however, recommend a reprint of the whole volume 'for there are many parts where the author falls into darkness and obscurity'. Nevertheless he found in Vaughan 'both feeling and imagination – flowers which not unfrequently show themselves above the weeds . . .'. The following eighteen-page article was largely taken up with long illustrative quotations from the secular verse. However, the work of Willmott and Lyte made this article a blind alley. Modern criticism has followed the judgement of the reverend editors, and has almost entirely neglected the secular verse.

The major achievement of the Victorians was to produce full-scale editions of the metaphysicals, culminating in the *Fuller Worthies'* editions of the 1870s, edited by the Reverend Alexander Grosart. By any modern standard of judgement, Grosart's editorial policy was unscholarly, but he did produce impressive

obtainable editions of, amongst others, the complete works of
Donne, Herbert, Vaughan, Crashaw and Marvell, each con-
taining extensive, pompous, but stimulating biographical and
critical introductions. In contrast with the editorial achievement
of Grosart, mid-nineteenth-century criticism made little advance.
The pattern was for critic after critic to go to the work of a metaphysical poet, express distaste at the poet's general style, and then
refer the reader to unexpected purple passages, using some such
image as gems among heaps of rubbish or wild flowers on
barren heaths. The habit continued until the end of the
century. Even from George Saintsbury, a critic whom Eliot
thought greatly responsible for the renewed interest in
seventeenth-century poetry, we find judgements as immature as
this, from his introduction to Donne's poems in 1896 :

It is seldom that even for a few lines, seldomer that for a few
stanzas, the power of the furnace is equal to the volumes of ore and
fuel that we thrust into it. But the fire is always there – over-tasked,
over-mastered for a time, but never choked or extinguished ; and ever
and anon from gaps in the smouldering mass there breaks forth
such a sudden flow of pure molten metal, such a flower of incan-
descence, as not even in the greatest poets of all can be ever surpassed
or often rivalled...

Similarly Edmund Gosse, the 1890s biographer of Donne,
punctuated his criticism, in this case from his *Jacobean Poets*
(1894), with observations that the reader may have to dig deep
for his poetic jewels :

. . . lovely sudden bursts of pure poetry . . . the most exquisite images
lie side by side with monstrous conceits and ugly pedantries. . . . For
us the charm of Donne continues to rest in his occasional felicities,
his bursts of melodious passion. . . . He pushes on with relentless
logic, – sometimes, indeed, past chains of images that are lovely and
appropriate ; but oftener through briars and hollows that rend his
garments and trip up his feet.

The inadequacies of Victorian criticism were most apparent in its treatment of Marvell and Herbert. Early responses to Captain Thomson's 1776 edition of Marvell had not been inauspicious. Charles Lamb, in *Essays of Elia*, praised Marvell highly. The *Retrospective Review* ran two articles packed with quotation, concluding with the belief that his works 'will one day attract the attention which, as part of the standard literature and history of our country, they so justly merit, and that day is not very far distant'. The prophecy, so far as Britain was concerned, was well off-centre. For the rest of the century Marvell was virtually ignored, the only major exception being Tennyson, who found a 'powerful union of pathos and humour' in 'To his Coy Mistress'. Marvell did find an audience, but in the United States. Edgar Allan Poe's response to 'The Nymph Complaining for the Death of Her Fawn' took up over two pages of an 1836 review of a poetry anthology. It was, he wrote, 'a beautiful poem, abounding in pathos, exquisitely delicate imagination and truthfulness'. Marvell received praise, too, from Whittier, Emerson and Lowell, and the first nineteenth-century edition of his poems appeared in Boston in 1857. This edition did not reach the British market until 1869.

Like Marvell's poems, Herbert's *Temple* found its best nineteenth-century critical audience in America (see Emerson's notes on pp. 67–70). English critics contented themselves with descriptions of Herbert the priest, the repetition of one or two of Coleridge's critical remarks, and then a final judgement on Herbert's 'quaintness'. Typical is the writer of an article in the *British Quarterly Review* in 1854, for whom even 'Vertue', Herbert's most 'romantic' poem, had grievous faults:

Even those exquisite lines, – 'Sweet day, so cool, so calm, so bright', – how are they spoilt by the next verse, where the very flower of beauty is addressed as :–

> Sweet rose, whose hue, angry and brave,
> Bids the bold gazer wipe his eye.

The rose angry! – the soft, rich colouring of its folded leaves painful to the sight! What but the strongest love of paradox could have imagined such a figure?

The dislike of conceits was carried over into the twentieth century. W. J. Courthope, in his *History of English Poetry* (1903), smugly suggested that Herbert 'cultivated quaintness for its own sake'; again 'Vertue' reveals the failure to respond to the verbal power of metaphysical verse :

Nor did he understand how great would be the feeling of artistic disappointment in the reader to find a poem on *Virtue* opening with the perfect stanza [*Quotes first stanza*] and concluding with this :–

> Only a sweet and virtuous soul,
> Like seasoned timber, never gives,
> And though the whole world turn to coal,
> Then chiefly lives.

I fear it is only too evident that Herbert was content to write 'coal' where he meant 'ash', because the latter word would not rhyme with 'soul'.

One, perhaps predictable, result of the refusal to accept the strengths of Herbert's verse was his relegation to the lowest ranks of the metaphysicals. Today the judgements seem bizarre. The *British Quarterly Review* article cited above finds in Quarles's *Emblemes* 'heights of noble poetry . . . which [Herbert] could never reach'. Less eccentric, but much more widespread, was the preference for Vaughan's verse above Herbert's.

Lyte's edition of Vaughan was the first to state such a preference. Vaughan's poetry, he wrote, had less of Herbert's 'quaint and fantastic turns, with a much larger infusion of poetic feeling and expression'. That too might have remained an eccentric judgement were it not for the development of a peculiar literary myth which made Vaughan one of the great influences upon Wordsworth. The first edition of the major Victorian anthology, Francis Palgrave's *Golden Treasury* (1861), contained Vaughan's poem 'The Retreate', with the note that 'Vaughan's beautiful though quaint verses should be compared with Wordsworth's "Ode" '. The ode in question was the 'Immortality Ode', and the critics seized upon the alleged resemblance. By 1869 resemblance had become influence when Archbishop Trench asserted, on no evidence at all, that Wordsworth had owned a copy of *Silex Scintillans*. The effect upon Vaughan's reputation was impressive – he became the first great poet of nature and childhood. In his edition of Vaughan's works, Grosart first quoted the 'Immortality Ode' in full, and then spent page after page demonstrating the superiority of Vaughan over Herbert, concluding triumphantly: 'Summarily I deny that Henry Vaughan was an imitator of George Herbert'. The apotheosis of Vaughan's fame came in Alice Meynell's judgement of 1910: '. . . the "Ode on Intimations of Immortality" is the work of Vaughan as much as of Wordsworth, or more than of Wordsworth. Vaughan not only set the sun of dreams in the heavens, he also set the child in the midst of humankind.'

IV

The 'revival' of metaphysical poetry in the years 1890–1923 may be best described as a return to the critical discrimination of Johnson and Coleridge. Impressionistic generalisations were replaced by a willingness to read the poetry closely, and on its own terms. Much of the credit for this went to T. S. Eliot but, with hindsight, we can see that his essay on the metaphysical poets was, more than anything else, propaganda for difficult poetry. The theory of the associated sensibility expressed neatly what critics had been saying about the metaphysicals since the turn of the century. Edith Sickel's words, in 1903, are very similar to Eliot's: 'All Vaughan's romance, indeed, lay in his intellect. Thought was with him an emotion and, when it wedded religion, he was at his highest. . . . About [Browning's] feelings there is a fine recklessness which Vaughan's *heart* could never know. But his *brain* knew it well and was tense enough in expressing it.' Three years later Herbert Grierson also used the comparison with Browning to convey the idea of the associated sensibility: 'There is nothing quite like Donne's love-poems in the language, except, perhaps, some of Browning's. Passion seems to affect both poets in the same way, not evoking the usual images, voluptuous and tender, but quickening the intellect to intense and rapid trains of thought. . . .'

Eliot's *dis*sociation of sensibility explained why 'poets in our civilisation . . . must be *difficult*', and he reinforced the point by a comparison with the French symbolist poets who had reached a method 'curiously similar to that of the "metaphysical poets" '. The analogy was in no way new – Gosse and Grierson had already made it – but it made a good defence for the kind of poetry Eliot was writing in the 1920s.

But Eliot's essay was, after all, only a review of Herbert Grierson's anthology, and beyond that essay he had little of interest to say about the metaphysical poets. They were a useful but limited weapon, soon superseded by the Jacobean dramatists and Dante. The great debt of twentieth-century criticism is owed to Grierson. His edition of Donne in 1912, and his anthology, *Metaphysical Lyrics and Poems of the Seventeenth Century*, in 1921 were, as Eliot said, as much works of criticism as collections of poems. Indeed Grierson's work in the period 1906–21 embodied much of the transition from Victorian to twentieth-century attitudes towards the metaphysicals. In 1906 he contributed a volume to Saintsbury's *Periods of European Literature*. There he carped at Donne's love poetry which contained 'too large an element . . . of mere intellectual subtlety, even freakishness'. The epithet for Herbert's poetry is familiar: 'quaint' is used four times in two pages to describe his treatment of themes, rhetoric, imagery and symbolism. Vaughan's best poetry is religious, and contains an 'occasional sublimity of imaginative vision to which Herbert never attained'. Worst of all is the treatment of Marvell – one page of generalisations, including the view that his poetry, contrasted with Vaughan's, is 'much more entirely descriptive and decorative'.

In the 1921 essay a much different picture is presented:

. . . the final effect of every poem of Donne's is a bizarre and blended one; but if the greatest poetry rises clear of the bizarre, the fantastic, yet very great poetry may be bizarre if it be the expression of a strangely blended temperament, an intense emotion, a vivid imagination. . . .

But the strongest personality of all is Andrew Marvell. . . at his very best a finer poet than [Donne or Dryden] . . . his few love poems and his few devotional pieces are perfect exponents of all the 'metaphysical' qualities – passionate, paradoxical argument, touched with humour and learned imagery. . . and above all the sudden roar of passion in bold and felicitous image. . . .

It is true that 'quaint' is used once in reference to Herbert, who is still thought inferior to Vaughan, but the whole essay is a masterpiece, as stimulating and effective as Johnson's 'Life of Cowley'.

In Grierson's anthology the nucleus of metaphysical poetry was seen to comprise the work of six poets: Donne (35 poems), Herbert (13), Vaughan (11), Marvell (10), Carew (10) and Crashaw (6). Helen Gardner's 1957 selection, *The Metaphysical Poets*, showed little change. Donne again led the way

(40 poems), followed by Herbert (24), Vaughan (17), Marvell (14), Carew (10) and Crashaw (9). In this century the critical reputations of Herbert, Vaughan and Marvell have benefited from their being, in one critic's phrase, 'on the coat-tails of Donne'. Crashaw and Carew have not fared so well. The 'metaphysical' tag has made them anthology poets, rarely the subject of studies in their own right, but usually providing an apt image or conceit to illustrate a general point about metaphysical poetry. Crashaw is still thought of as essentially foreign, despite impressive studies of his style and poetic development in the 1930s by Ruth Wallerstein and Austin Warren. Carew's status as a minor poet has not been affected by F. R. Leavis's projection of a line of wit in which he stands as an important link between Jonson and Donne on the one hand, and Marvell and Pope on the other.

The twentieth-century revival has resolutely ignored those metaphysical poets who had been most popular in the second half of the seventeenth century. Cowley's reputation underwent a long decline in the nineteenth century. In the *Cornhill Magazine* in 1876 Gosse described how he had come to Cowley's work out of sheer interest in the unknown – he had wanted to know 'why Cowley ever attained so immense a reputation, and why having once gained it, he has so completely lost it'. The following survey of Cowley's poetry was unsympathetic. The greatest contempt was reserved for *The Mistress* which Gosse found scarcely readable, 'too ridiculous for quotation . . . and set to eccentric measures . . . that but serve to prove his metrical ineptitude'. Only the elegies on Hervey and Crashaw were really worth preserving, and Gosse saw himself as the last of Cowley's admirers. The article perhaps did more to demonstrate Gosse's failure to understand the strengths of metaphysical poetry, but later critics have been only a little more charitable. Cowley now seems to represent the death of the metaphysical tradition :

The fashion of 'metaphysical' wit remains in Cowley's poems when
the spirit that gave it colour and music is gone.

(Herbert Grierson)

The intensity of Donne is passing away in Cowley, and the long
struggle between reason and imagination is coming to a close in the
victory of reason and good sense.

(George Williamson)

Unlike Cowley, Quarles maintained his popularity throughout the nineteenth century, with at least twelve editions of his
Emblemes up to 1888 (despite Lamb's lament 'O tempora! O
lectores!' at finding a remaindered copy at a book-stall). This
century has virtually ignored him – 'Quarles hardly belongs to
the "metaphysical" tradition' was Grierson's view – and his only
interest now is to students of emblem books.

The third neglected poet is Cleveland. He had been at one
stage the most popular of all, inspiring the most grandiloquent
praise: witness S.H.'s funeral elegy, where Cleveland is des-
scribed as a 'great Gargantuan, huge Colossian bard'. S.H.
continues:

> Who shall dare sing thy worth unlesse prepar'd
> With Sack and Sulphure, every word should pierce
> Like Thunder through the wond'ring Universe;
> Although thou art inhum'd (to fancy Fate)
> Yet still to us thou dost tonitruate,
> Thy words want each an Atlas; we can Rant,
> 'Tis true, but not like thee (our Termagant)
> Whose every syllable a sentence is,
> Each word an Axiome. . .

Both the object of S.H.'s praise, and the way that praise is expressed, are entirely alien to us. Nothing illustrates more clearly
the selectivity of our metaphysical revival.

V

T. S. Eliot brought Cleveland's name into an article he wrote on
Donne in 1923. The context is interesting in its implications for
modern criticism : 'But, meanwhile, those who take Donne as a
contemporary will be taking him as a fashion only. Neither the
fantastic (Clevelandism is becoming popular) nor the cynical
nor the sensual occupies an excessive importance with Donne.'
Much of Eliot's later lukewarmness towards the metaphysicals
came from the fact that they were no longer a difficult, acquired
taste, but were fast being used as a standard of comparison for
all poetry. 'Metaphysical' became not so much descriptive as
evaluative. Genevieve Taggard's anthology *Circumference*
(1929) saw in metaphysical poetry a state of mind common to
the best poetry of all ages. Her examples of metaphysical verse
included, as well as the seventeenth-century poets, poems by
Dunbar, Byrd, Sidney, Pope, Gray, Blake, Emily Dickinson, e. e.
cummings and T. S. Eliot. Her hopes were that the greatest
metaphysical poetry had yet to be written :

For the metaphysical poet, Science is the freedom of the universe –
and in the future our greatest poets may well be poets of this mind.
Some Moses striking a rock on the desert Mr. Eliot describes as the
wasteland and with his touch liberating a vast unused mentality;
the excitement of enormous sweeps, the dizziness of looking in all
directions at the surrounding fact.

Miss Taggard's scientific poetry is still unwritten. The science of
literary criticism has, however, found in metaphysical poetry an
ideal testing-ground for theory and practice. The extracts in
the modern section of this Casebook have been chosen as much for
their difference of approach, as for their various conceptions of
what constitutes metaphysical poetry.

First and foremost is Rosemond Tuve's *Elizabethan and Metaphysical Imagery* (1947). The extract on the 'Criterion of Decorum' comes from half-way through her study of sixteenth- and seventeenth-century poetic theory, a work which demanded and brought about a salutary revision of critical attitudes towards Renaissance poetry. S. L. Bethell's 'The Nature of Metaphysical Wit' (1953) is one of the many fine studies inspired by Rosemund Tuve's book. Bethell sets out to supplement and rectify her account of metaphysical wit, using her methods and ends, by applying the results of his researches to Donne's 'The Flea'.

In contrast with the work of Tuve and Bethell is Leo Spitzer's analysis of Donne's 'The Extasie', part of a larger essay, 'Three Poems on Ecstasy' (1949). Spitzer developed his method of *explication de textes* in studies of continental literature, and came to apply it to English poetry late in life. Imagery, for Spitzer, was relatively unimportant. His method was to look closely at details of language and style, and then to work inductively towards an interpretation of the poem.

The essays on individual poems – Joseph Summers on Herbert, and Rosalie Colie on Marvell – represent two contrasting schools of criticism. Joseph Summers's book, *George Herbert: His Religion and Art* (1954), is a non-polemical study of Herbert's life, religion and poetry, aimed at giving the reader the essential materials 'to recognise a good poem'. Rosalie Colie's book on Marvell, *My Ecchoing Song* (1970), concentrates entirely on the poetry, and attempts to demonstrate how Marvell 'sums up, examines, and questions the traditions he inherited'. Earl Miner's 'Alteration of Time', from his *The Metaphysical Mode from Donne to Cowley* (1969), treats mainly the poetry of Vaughan and Cowley. Miner's book is a particularly discriminating study of the features which constitute metaphysical style, and the differences possible within that style.

Finally, the joker in the pack is the essay by Josephine Miles and Hanan Selvin : a tentative application of the computer to seventeenth-century poetic language. Miles and Selvin are not concerned solely with the metaphysicals, but their results throw an interesting light on the assumption that there is such a race.

PART ONE

Seventeenth- and Eighteenth-Century Criticism

Thomas Sprat

. . . If any shall think that [Cowley] was not wonderfully curious in the choice and elegance of all his words, I will affirm with more truth on the other side, that he had no manner of affectation in them : he took them as he found them made to his hands; he neither went before nor came after the use of the Age. He forsook the Conversation, but never the Language, of the City and Court. He understood exceeding well all the variety and power of Poetical Numbers, and practis'd all sorts with great happiness. If his Verses in some place seem not as soft and flowing as some would have them, it was his choice, not his fault. He knew that in diverting mens minds there should be the same variety observ'd as in the prospects of their Eyes, where a Rock, a Precipice, or a rising Wave is often more delightful than a smooth, even ground or a calm Sea. Where the matter required it, he was as gentle as any man. But where higher Virtues were chiefly to be regarded, an exact numerosity was not then his main care. This may serve to answer those who upbraid some of his Pieces with roughness, and with more contractions than they are willing to allow. But these Admirers of gentlenesse without sinews should know that different Arguments must have different Colours of Speech : that there is a kind of variety of Sexes in Poetry as well as in Mankind : that as the peculiar excellence of the Feminine Kind is smoothnesse and beauty, so strength is the chief praise of the Masculine. . . .

If any are displeas'd at the boldness of his Metaphors and length of his Digressions they contend not against Mr. *Cowley*, but *Pindar* himself. . . . If the irregularity of the number disgust them, they may observe that this very thing makes that kind of Poesie fit for all manner of subjects: For the Pleasant, the Grave, the Amorous, the Heroic, the Philosophical, the Moral, the Divine. Besides this they will find that the frequent alteration of the Rhythm and Feet affects the mind with a more various delight, while it is soon apt to be tyr'd by the setled pace of any one constant measure. But that for which I think this inequality of number is chiefly to be preferr'd is its near affinity with Prose: From which all other kinds of *English* Verse are so far distant that it is very seldom found that the same Man excels in both ways. But now this loose and unconfin'd measure has all the Grace and Harmony of the most Confin'd. And withal it is so large and free, that the practice of it will only exalt, not corrupt our Prose, which is certainly the most useful kind of Writing of all others, for it is the style of all business and conversation.

S o u r c e : *An Account of the Life and Writings of Mr Abraham Cowley* (1668).

Edward Phillips

George Herbert . . . produced those so generally known and approved Poems entitled the Temple. . . .

John Cleaveland, a Notable Highsoaring Witty Loyalist of *Cambridge* . . . In fine, so great a Man hath *Cleaveland* been in the Estimation of the generality, in regard his Conceits were out of the common road, and Wittily farfetch't, that Grave Men, in outward appearance have not spar'd in my hearing to affirm him the best of English Poets, and let them think so still, who ever please, provided it be made no Article of Faith.

John Donne . . . the sharpness of his Wit, and gayety of Fancy . . . in which state of life he compos'd his more brisk and Youthful Poems, which are rather commended for the heighth of Fancy and acuteness of conceit, than for the Smoothness of the Verse. . . .

Francis Quarles, the darling of our Plebian Judgments, that is such as have ingenuity enough to delight in Poetry, but are not sufficiently instructed to make a right choice and distinction.

Thomas Carew . . . was reckon'd among the Chiefest of his time for delicacy of wit and Poetic Fancy, by the strength of which his extant Poems still maintain their fame amidst the Curious of the present Age.

SOURCE: *Theatrum Poetarum Anglicanorum* (1674).

William Winstanley

Doctor John Donne: This pleasant Poet, painful Preacher, and pious Person....

Richard Crashaw . . . a religious pourer forth of his divine Raptures and Meditations, in smooth and pathetick Verse . . .; such rich pregnant Fancies as shewed his Breast to be filled with *Phoeban* Fire....

John Cleveland: This eminent Poet, the Wit of our age. . . . His Epistles were pregnant with Metaphors, carrying in them a difficult plainness, difficult at the hearing, plain at the considering thereof. His lofty Fancy may seem to stride from the top of one Mountain to the top of another, so making to it self a constant level and Champian of continued Elevations.

Such who have Clevelandiz'd, that is, endeavoured to imitate his Masculine stile, yet could never go beyond his Poem of the Hermaphrodite . . . [it] hath in it the very *vein* and strain of Mr *Cleveland's* writing, walking from one height to another, in a constant level of continued Elevation....

. . . among the rest one made this Anagram upon his name:

JOHN CLEAVELAND

HELICONIAN DEW

SOURCE: *The Lives of the Most Famous English Poets* (1687). The comments on Cleveland are largely repeated from Fuller's *History of the Worthies of England* (1662).

Giles Jacob

Abraham Cowley . . . our *English Pindar*. . . . [His *Mistress*] shews the prodigious wit of the Author, beyond any Poetry ever printed in the *English* Tongue.

Thomas Carew . . . the Author of several *Love Poems* which met with Approbation, but he is very Wanton in some of them, and has carried his Flight to an Extravagancy.

SOURCE: *The Poetical Register* (1723).

Anonymous (1697)

Mr Herbert's *Poems* have met with so general and deserv'd Acceptance, that they have undergone Eleven Impressions near Twenty Years ago: He hath obtain'd by way of Eminency, the Name of *Our Divine Poet*, and his Verses have been frequently quoted in Sermons and other Discourses; yet, I fear, few of them have been Sung since his Death, the Tunes not being at the Command of ordinary Readers.

This attempt therefore, (such as it is) is to bring so many of them as I well could, which I judg'd suited to the Capacity and Devotion of Private Christians, into the *Common Metre* to be Sung in their Closets or Families. . . .

How much more fit is *Herbert's Temple* to be set to the Lute, than *Cowley's Mistress*! It is hard that no one can be taught Musick, but in such wanton Songs as fill the Hearts of many Learners with Lust and Vanity all their Days. . . . My attempt hath been easie, only to alter the measures of some Hymns, keeping strictly to the Sence of the Author; But how noble an undertaking were it, if any one could and would rescue the high flights, and lofty strains found in the most Celebrated Poets, from their sacrilegious Applications to *Carnal Love*, and restore them to the *Divine Love*! . . .

Almost all Phrases and Expressions of Worship due only to God, are continu'd in these artificial Composures in the Heathenish use of them, even from the *inspirations* that they invoke in their beginning, to the *Raptures, Flames, Adorations,* &c. That they pretend to in the Progress: Nor are these meer empty Names with them, but their Hearts are more fervently carried out in the musical use of them, than they would be if their Knees were bow'd to *Baal* and *Astaroth*: Few Holy Souls are more affected with the Praises of a Redeemer, than they are of the wanton Object that they profess to adore. Oh for some to write *Parodies*, by which Name I find one Poem in *Herbert* call'd, which begins, *Souls Joy, where art thou gone*, and was, I doubt not, a light Love-song turn'd into a Spiritual Hymn. . . . I do not find it hath been made a Matter of scruple to turn the Temples built for Idols into Churches: And as to this Case, it is to be consider'd that the Musick and Poetry was an excellent Gift of God, which ought to have been us'd for Him; and that their high strains of Love, Joy, &c. Suit none but the adorable Saviour; and all their most warm and affecting Expressions are stollen from the Churches Adoration of Christ; and who can doubt but the Church may take her own, whereever she finds it, whether in an Idolatrous Mass-Book or Prophane Love-song?

S o u r c e : *Select Hymns Taken out of Mr Herbert's Temple*
  (1697).

Joseph Addison

Mr *Lock* has an admirable Reflection upon the Difference of Wit and Judgment, whereby he endeavours to shew the Reason why they are not always the Talents of the same Person. His Words are as follows: *And hence, perhaps, may be given some Reason of that common Observation, That Men who have a great deal of Wit and prompt Memories, have not always the clearest Judgment, or deepest Reason. For Wit lying most in the Assemblage of Ideas, and putting those together with Quickness and Variety, wherein can be found any Resemblance or Congruity thereby to make up pleasant Pictures and agreeable Visions in the Fancy; Judgment, on the contrary, lies quite on the other Side, In separating carefully one from another, Ideas wherein can be found the least Difference, thereby to avoid being misled by Similitude and by Affinity to take one thing for another. This is a Way of proceeding quite contrary to Metaphor and Allusion; wherein, for the most Part, lies that Entertainment and Pleasantry of Wit which strikes so lively on the Fancy, and is therefore so acceptable to all People.*

This is, I think, the best and most philosophical Account that I have ever met with of Wit, which generally, tho' not always, consists in such a Resemblance and Congruity of Ideas as this Author mentions. I shall only add to it, by way of Explanation, That every Resemblance of Ideas is not that which we call Wit, unless it be such an one that gives *Delight* and *Surprize* to the Reader: These two Properties seem essential to Wit, more particularly the last of them. In order therefore that the

Resemblance in the Ideas be Wit, it is necessary that the Ideas should not lie too near one another in the Nature of things; for where the Likeness is obvious, it gives no Surprize. To compare one Man's Singing to that of another, or to represent the Whiteness of any Object by that of Milk and Snow, or the Variety of its Colours by those of the Rainbow, cannot be called Wit, unless, besides this obvious Resemblance, there be some further Congruity discovered in the two Ideas that is capable of giving the Reader some Surprize. Thus when a Poet tells us, the Bosom of his Mistress is as white as Snow, there is no Wit in the Comparison; but when he adds, with a Sigh, that it is as cold too, it then grows into Wit. Every Reader's Memory may supply him with innumerable Instances of the same Nature. For this Reason, the Similitudes in Heroick Poets, who endeavour rather to fill the Mind with great Conceptions, than to divert it with such as are new and surprizing, have seldom any thing in them that can be called Wit. Mr *Lock*'s Account of Wit, with this short Explanation, comprehends most of the Species of Wit, as Metaphors, Similitudes, Allegories, Ænigmas, Mottos, Parables, Fables, Dreams, Visions, dramatick Writings, Burlesque, and all the Methods of Allusion : As there are many other Pieces of Wit (how remote soever they may appear at first Sight from the foregoing Description) which upon Examination will be found to agree with it.

As *true Wit* generally consists in this Resemblance and Congruity of Ideas, *false Wit* chiefly consists in the Resemblance and Congruity sometimes of single Letters, as in Anagrams, Chronograms, Lipograms, and Acrosticks : Sometimes of Syllables, as in Ecchos and Doggerel Rhymes : Sometimes of Words, as in Punns and Quibbles; and sometimes of whole Sentences or Poems, cast into the Figures of *Eggs, Axes,* or *Altars* : Nay some carry the Notion of Wit so far, as to ascribe it even to external Mimickry; and to look upon a Man as an ingenious Person, that can resemble the Tone, Posture, or Face of another.

As *true Wit* consists in the Resemblance of Ideas, and *false Wit* in the Resemblance of Words, according to the foregoing Instances; there is another kind of Wit which consists partly in the Resemblance of Ideas, and partly in the Resemblance of Words; which for Distinction Sake I shall call *mixt Wit*. This Kind of Wit is that which abounds in *Cowley*, more than in any Author that ever wrote. Mr *Waller* has likewise a great deal of it. Mr *Dryden* is very sparing in it. *Milton* had a Genius much above it. *Spencer* is in the same Class with *Milton*. The *Italians*, even in their Epic Poetry, are full of it. Monsieur *Boileau*, who formed himself upon the ancient Poets, has every where rejected it with Scorn. If we look after mixt Wit among the *Greek* Writers, we shall find it no where but in the Epigrammatists. There are indeed some Strokes of it in the little Poem ascribed to *Musæus*, which by that, as well as many other Marks, betrays it self to be a modern Composition. If we look into the *Latin* Writers, we find none of this mixt Wit in *Virgil, Lucretius,* or *Catullus*; very little in *Horace*, but a great deal of it in *Ovid*, and scarce any thing else in *Martial.*

Out of the innumerable Branches of mixt Wit, I shall chuse one Instance which may be met with in all the Writers of this Class. The Passion of Love in its Nature has been thought to resemble Fire; for which Reason the Words Fire and Flame are made use of to signify Love. The witty Poets therefore have taken an Advantage from the doubtful Meaning of the Word Fire, to make an infinite Number of Witticisms. *Cowley* observing the cold Regard of his Mistress's Eyes, and at the same Time their Power of producing Love in him, considers them as Burning-Glasses made of Ice; and finding himself able to live in the greatest Extremities of Love, concludes the Torrid Zone to be habitable. When his Mistress has read his Letter written in Juice of Lemmon by holding it to the Fire, he desires her to read it over a second time by Love's Flames. When she weeps, he wishes it were inward Heat that distilled those Drops from the Limbeck. When she is absent he is beyond eighty, that is, thirty Degrees nearer the Pole than when she is with him. His ambitious Love is a Fire that naturally mounts upwards, his happy Love is the Beams of Heaven, and his unhappy Love Flames of Hell. When it does not let him sleep, it is a Flame that sends up no Smoak; when it is opposed by Counsel and Advice, it is a Fire that rages the more by the Wind's blowing upon it. Upon the dying of a Tree in which he had cut his Loves, he observes that his written Flames had burnt up and withered the Tree. When he resolves to give over his Passion, he tells us that one burnt like him for ever dreads the Fire. His Heart is an *Ætna*, that instead of *Vulcan*'s Shop encloses *Cupid*'s Forge in it. His endeavouring to drown his Love in Wine, is throwing Oil upon the Fire. He would insinuate to his Mistress, that the Fire of Love, like that of the Sun (which produces so many living Creatures) should not only warm but beget. Love in another Place cooks Pleasure at his Fire. Sometimes the Poet's Heart is frozen in every Breast, and sometimes scorched in every Eye. Sometimes he is drowned in Tears, and burnt in Love, like a Ship set on fire in the Middle of the Sea.

The Reader may observe in every one of these Instances, that the Poet mixes the Qualities of Fire with those of Love; and in the same Sentence speaking of it both as a Passion and as real Fire, surprizes the Reader with those seeming Resemblances or Contradictions that make up all the Wit in this kind of Writing. Mixt Wit therefore is a Composition of Punn and true Wit, and is more or less perfect as the Resemblance lies in the Ideas or in the Words: Its Foundations are laid partly in Falsehood and partly in Truth: Reason puts in her Claim for one Half of it, and Extravagance for the other. The only Province therefore for this kind of Wit, is Epigram, or those little occasional Poems that in their own Nature are nothing else but a Tissue of Epigrams. I cannot conclude this Head of *mixt Wit*, without owning that the admirable Poet out of whom I have taken the Examples of it, had as much true Wit as any Author that ever writ; and indeed all other Talents of an extraordinary Genius. . . .

SOURCE: *The Spectator*, LXII (1711).

John Oldmixon

. . . The noble Critick plainly alludes to the punning sermons in the Reign of King James I, and the Metaphysical Love-verses by which *Donne* and *Cowley* acquir'd so much Fame. Cowley, especially, with as much Wit as ever Man had, shews as little Judgment, by which his Poetry in our Days so sunk in the Opinion of good Judges, that there is no Hope of its rising again. . . .

But those Wits that subtilize, need only follow their Genius to take Flight, and lose themselves in their own Thoughts. Dr *Donne*, and Mr *Cowley* are sufficient Instances of this Vice in our Language: the Latter, as has been hinted, copy'd the Former in his Faults; and it seems strange to me, that after *Suckling* and *Waller* had written, whose Genius's were so fine and just, Mr *Cowley* should imitate Dr *Donne*, in whom there's hardly any Thing that's agreeable, or one Stroke which has any Likeness to Nature. . . .

[Quotes 'Our two souls therefore which are one']

What Woman's Heart in the World could stand out against such an Attack as this, after she once understood how to handle a Pair of Compasses? Both *Donne* and *Cowley* were Men of Learning, and must consequently have read the Ancients over and over. They could never learn this from them, but owe all the Extravagence in it to their own Genius's.

The learned Jesuit told us that the younger *Pliny* endeavoured to be witty upon all Things in Season and out of Season. The same may be said of *Cowley*, not excepting his *Mistress*, tho' Affectation in Love-Verses is most inexcusable: Love is the

Darling-Child of Nature, and is as much inconsistent with Affectation as Passion is with Simile. In Love-Verses it is most easily avoided. For let the Heart but speak, and it will carry Infection with it. When the Head is playing Tricks, the Heart of the fair One will ever be insensible; and then a Man may as well crack Jests to a Judge, as a Lover be witty to his Mistress.

SOURCE: *The Arts of Logick and Rhetorick* (1728).

Anonymous (1762)

. . . There [Italy] likewise they pretended to a sort of lyric poetry, under the name of sonnets and madrigals, which, being founded upon the metaphysical quibbling then in vogue, instead of the truth of passion and sentiment, was wholly made up of jingling expressions, that, with much subtlety, kept up a seeming relation betwixt thoughts, in themselves, not at all akin. A sort of writing, though called by some people to this day *wit*, much inferior to fair punning; as it equally trifles with the understanding, without the merit of shaking the sides. . . .

At last the Revolution [of 1688]. . . . Metaphysics now no longer necessary in support of opinions which were now no longer useful in the acquisition of power and riches, sunk by degrees into contempt; and Nature, having at last shewn her true and beautiful face, poetry, from acting the part of a magic lanthorn teeming with monsters and chimeras, resumed her genuine province, like the camera obscura, of reflecting the things that are. . . .

At this very day, when few men take the trouble of becoming very learned, and fewer give to the public any proofs of their poetic fire, the taste acquired by the last age in certain kinds of poetry, still continues; and the most insipid odes, that appear in the magazines, are better able to stand a critical discussion than those that were written by the brightest wits a hundred years ago.

SOURCE: *A Dialogue on Taste* (1762).

Samuel Johnson

Cowley, like other poets who have written with narrow views and, instead of tracing intellectual pleasure to its natural sources in the mind of man, paid their court to temporary prejudices, has been at one time too much praised and too much neglected at another.

Wit, like all other things subject by their nature to the choice of man, has its changes and fashions, and at different times takes different forms. About the beginning of the seventeenth century appeared a race of writers that may be termed the metaphysical poets, of whom in a criticism on the works of Cowley it is not improper to give some account.

The metaphysical poets were men of learning, and to shew their learning was their whole endeavour; but, unluckily resolving to shew it in rhyme, instead of writing poetry they only wrote verses, and very often such verses as stood the trial of the finger better than of the ear; for the modulation was so imperfect that they were only found to be verses by counting the syllables.

If the father of criticism has rightly denominated poetry τέχνη μιμητική, *an imitative art*, these writers will without great wrong lose their right to the name of poets, for they cannot be said to have imitated any thing : they neither copied nature nor life; neither painted the forms of matter nor represented the operations of intellect.

Those however who deny them to be poets allow them to be wits. Dryden confesses of himself and his contemporaries that they fall below Donne in wit, but maintains that they surpass him in poetry.

If Wit be well described by Pope as being 'that which has been often thought, but was never before so well expressed', they certainly never attained nor ever sought it, for they endeavoured to be singular in their thoughts, and were careless of their diction. But Pope's account of wit is undoubtedly erroneous; he depresses it below its natural dignity, and reduces it from strength of thought to happiness of language.

If by a more noble and more adequate conception that be considered as Wit which is at once natural and new, that which though not obvious is, upon its first production, acknowledged to be just; if it be that, which he that never found it, wonders how he missed; to wit of this kind the metaphysical poets have seldom risen. Their thoughts are often new, but seldom natural; they are not obvious, but neither are they just; and the reader, far from wondering that he missed them, wonders more frequently by what perverseness of industry they were ever found.

But Wit, abstracted from its effects upon the hearer, may be more rigorously and philosophically considered as a kind of *discordia concors*; a combination of dissimilar images, or discovery of occult resemblances in things apparently unlike. Of wit, thus defined, they have more than enough. The most heterogeneous ideas are yoked by violence together; nature and art are ransacked for illustrations, comparisons, and allusions; their learning instructs, and their subtilty surprises; but the reader commonly thinks his improvement dearly bought, and, though he sometimes admires, is seldom pleased.

From this account of their compositions it will be readily inferred that they were not successful in representing or moving the affections. As they were wholly employed on something unexpected and surprising they had no regard to that uniformity of

sentiment, which enables us to conceive and to excite the pains
and the pleasure of other minds: they never enquired what on
any occasion they should have said or done, but wrote rather as
beholders than partakers of human nature; as beings looking
upon good and evil, impassive and at leisure; as Epicurean
deities making remarks on the actions of men and the vicissitudes
of life, without interest and without emotion. Their courtship was
void of fondness and their lamentation of sorrow. Their wish was
only to say what they hoped had been never said before.

Nor was the sublime more within their reach than the pathetick; for they never attempted that comprehension and expanse of
thought which at once fills the whole mind, and of which the
first effect is sudden astonishment, and the second rational admiration. Sublimity is produced by aggregation, and littleness by
dispersion. Great thoughts are always general, and consist in
positions not limited by exceptions, and in descriptions not des-
cending to minuteness. It is with great propriety that subtlety,
which in its original import means exility of particles, is taken in
its metaphorical meaning for nicety of distinction. Those writers
who lay on the watch for novelty could have little hope of greatness; for great things cannot have escaped former observation.
Their attempts were always analytick: they broke every image
into fragments, and could no more represent by their slender
conceits and laboured particularities the prospects of nature or
the scenes of life, than he who dissects a sun-beam with a prism
can exhibit the wide effulgence of a summer noon.

What they wanted however of the sublime they endeavoured
to supply by hyperbole; their amplification had no limits: they
left not only reason but fancy behind them, and produced com-
binations of confused magnificence that not only could not be
credited, but could not be imagined.

Yet great labour directed by great abilities is never wholly
lost: if they frequently threw away their wit upon false con-

ceits, they likewise sometimes struck out unexpected truth : if their conceits were far-fetched, they were often worth the carriage. To write on their plan it was at least necessary to read and think. No man could be born a metaphysical poet, nor assume the dignity of a writer by descriptions copied from descriptions, by imitations borrowed from imitations, by traditional imagery and hereditary similes, by readiness of rhyme and volubility of syllables.

In perusing the works of this race of authors the mind is exercised either by recollection or inquiry; either something already learned is to be retrieved, or something new is to be examined. If their greatness seldom elevates their acuteness often surprises; if the imagination is not always gratified, at least the powers of reflection and comparison are employed; and in the mass of materials, which ingenious absurdity has thrown together, genuine wit and useful knowledge may be sometimes found, buried perhaps in grossness of expression, but useful to those who know their value, and such as, when they are expanded to perspicuity and polished to elegance, may give lustre to works which have more propriety though less copiousness of sentiment.

This kind of writing, which was, I believe, borrowed from Marino and his followers, had been recommended by the example of Donne, a man of very extensive and various knowledge, and by Jonson, whose manner resembled that of Donne more in the ruggedness of his lines than in the cast of his sentiments.

When their reputation was high they had undoubtedly more imitators than time has left behind. Their immediate successsors, of whom any remembrance can be said to remain, were Suckling, Waller, Denham, Cowley, Cleiveland, and Milton. Denham and Waller sought another way to fame, by improving the harmony of our numbers. Milton tried the metaphysick style only in his lines upon Hobson the Carrier. Cowley adopted it, and excelled his predecessors; having as much sentiment and more musick. Suckling neither improved versification nor abounded in conceits. The fashionable style remained chiefly with Cowley: Suckling could not reach it, and Milton disdained it.

SOURCE: *Lives of the Poets – Abraham Cowley* (1779).

PART TWO

Nineteenth- and Early Twentieth-Century Criticism

Samuel Coleridge

Doubtless, all the copies I have ever seen of Donne's Poems are grievously misprinted. Wonderful that they are not more so, considering that not one in a thousand of his readers have any notion how his lines are to be read – to the many, five out of six appear anti-metrical. How greatly this aided the compositor's negligence or ignorance, and prevented the corrector's remedy, any man may ascertain by examining the earliest editions of blank verse plays. Massinger, Beaumont and Fletcher, &c. Now, Donne's rhythm was as inexplicable to the many as blank verse, spite of his rhymes – ergo, as blank verse, misprinted. I am convinced that where no mode of rational declamation by pause, hurrying of voice, or apt and sometimes double emphasis, can at once make the verse metrical and bring out the sense of passion more prominently, that there we are entitled to alter the text, when it can be done by simple omission or addition of *that, which, and*, and such 'small deer'; or by mere placing of the same words – I would venture nothing beyond.

> And by delighting many, frees again
> Grief which Verse did restrain.
> 'The Triple Fool', v. 15

A good instance how Donne read his own verses. We should write 'The Grief, verse did restrain'; but Donne roughly emphasized the two main words, Grief and Verse, and, therefore, made each the first syllable of a trochee or dactyl : –

Grief, which / verse did re / strain
And we join to't our strength,
And we teach it art and length.

*

TO CANONIZATION

One of my favourite poems. As late as ten years ago, I used to
seek and find out grand lines and fine stanzas; but my delight
has been far greater since it has consisted more in tracing the
leading thought thro'out the whole. The former is too much like
coveting your neighbor's goods; in the latter you merge yourself
in the author, you *become He*.

*

The vividness of the descriptions or declamations in DONNE,
or DRYDEN, is as much and as often derived from the force and
fervour of the describer, as from the reflections forms or
incidents which constitute their subject and materials. The wheels
take fire from the mere rapidity of their motion.

*

FRANCIS QUARLES

Unusually great earnestness, intension and devotion to any one
thing in and for itself necesarily weakens or precludes the dis-
turbing force of associations. Quarles, Withers, and others have
been unkindly underrated on this account – their want of

Taste was from fullness of Appetite, their sound Hunger and Thirst after religion.

*

Quarles' Emblems – Even in the present Rage for our old poets, how much under-rated!

*

G E O R G E   H E R B E R T

I find more substantial comfort now in pious George Herbert's *Temple*, which I used to read to amuse myself with his quaintness, in short, only to laugh at, than in all the poetry since the poems of Milton. If you have not read Herbert I can recommend the book to you confidently. The poem entitled 'The Flower' is especially affecting; and to me such a phrase as 'and relish versing' expresses a sincerity and reality, which I would willingly exchange for the more dignified 'and once more love the Muse', &c. and so with many other of Herbert's homely phrases.

*

G. Herbert is a true poet, but a poet *sui generis*, the merits of whose poems will never be felt without a sympathy with the mind and character of the man. To appreciate this volume, it is not enough that the reader possesses a cultivated judgment, classical taste, or even poetic sensibility, unless he be likewise a *Christian*, and both a zealous and an orthodox, both a devout and a *devotional* Christian. But even this will will not quite suffice. He must be an affectionate and dutiful child of the Church, and from habit, conviction, and a constitutional predisposition to ceremoniousness, in piety as in manners, find her forms and ordinances aids of religion, not sources of formality; for religion is the element in which he lives, and the region in which he moves.

*

Every time I read Herbert anew, the more he grows in my liking. I admire him greatly. – 14 June 1826.

*

My dear old friend Charles Lamb and I differ widely (and in point of taste and moral feeling this is a rare occurrence) in our estimation and liking of George Herbert's sacred poems. He greatly prefers Quarles, nay, he *dis*likes Herbert. But if Herbert had only written the two following stanzas[1] – and there are a hundred other that in one mood or other of my mind have impressed me – I should be grateful for the possession of his works. The stanzas are especially affecting to me; because the folly of overvaluing myself in any reference to my future lot is *not* the sin or danger that besets me, but a tendency to self-contempt, a sense of the utter disproportionateness of all I can call *me*, to the promises of the Gospel – *this* is *my* sorest temptation : the promises, I say, not to the *threats*. For in order to the fulfilment of these, it needs only that I should be left to myself to sink into the chaos and lawless productivity of my own still perishing yet imperishable nature.

S o u r c e : Roberta Florence Brinkley (ed.), *Coleridge on the Seventeenth Century*; taken from notes and letters written between 1811 and 1826.

NOTE

1. These are not given in the source.

William Hazlitt

The writers here referred to (such as Donne, Davies, Crashaw, and others) not merely mistook learning for poetry – they thought any thing was poetry that differed from ordinary prose and the natural impression of things, by being intricate, far-fetched, and improbable. Their style was not so properly learned as metaphysical; that is to say, whenever, by any violence done to their ideas, they could make out an abstract likeness or possible ground of comparison, they forced the image, whether learned or vulgar, into the service of the Muses. Any thing would do to 'hitch into a rhyme', no matter whether striking or agreeable, or not, so that it would puzzle the reader to discover the meaning, and if there was the most remote circumstance, however trifling or vague, for the pretended comparison to hinge upon. They brought ideas together not the most, but the least like; and of which the collision produced not light, but obscurity – served not to strengthen, but to confound. Their mystical verses read like riddles or an allegory. They neither belong to the class of lively or severe poetry. They have not the force of the one, nor the gaiety of the other; but are an ill-assorted, unprofitable union of the two together, applying to serious subjects that quaint and partial style of allusion which fits only what is light and ludicrous, and building the most laboured conclusions on the most fantastical and slender premises. The object of the poetry of imagination is to raise or adorn one idea by another more striking or more beautiful: the object of these writers was to match any one idea with any other idea, *for better for worse*, as we say, and whether any thing was gained by the change of condition or not. The object of the poetry of the passions again is to illustrate any strong feeling, by shewing the same feeling as connected with objects or circumstances more palpable and touching; but here the object was to strain and distort the immediate feeling into some barely possible consequence or recondite analogy, in which it required the utmost stretch of misapplied ingenuity to trace the smallest connection with the original impression. In short, the poetry of this period was strictly the poetry not of ideas, but of *definitions*: it proceeded in mode and figure, by *genus* and specific difference; and was the logic of the schools, or an oblique and forced construction of dry, literal matter-of-fact, decked out in a robe of glittering conceits, and clogged with the halting shackles of verse. The imagination of the writers, instead of being conversant with the face of nature, or the secrets of the heart, was lost in the labyrinths of intellectual abstraction, or entangled in the technical quibbles and impertinent intricacies of language. The complaint so often made, and here repeated, is not of the want of power in these men, but of the waste of it; not of the absence of genius, but the abuse of it. They had (many of them) great talents committed to their trust, richness of thought, and depth of feeling; but they chose to hide them (as much as they possibly could) under a false shew of learning and unmeaning subtlety. From the style which they had systematically adopted, they thought nothing done till they had perverted simplicity into affectation, and spoiled nature by art. They seemed to think there was an irreconcileable opposition between genius, as well as grace, and nature; tried to do without, or else constantly to thwart her; left nothing to her outward 'impress', or spontaneous impulses, but made a point of twisting and torturing almost every subject they took in hand, till they had fitted it to the mould of their self-opinion and the previous fabrications of their own fancy, like those who pen acrostics in the shape of pyramids, and cut out trees into the shape of peacocks. Their chief aim is to make you wonder at the writer, not to interest you in the subject; and by an incessant craving after admiration, they have lost what they might have gained with less extravagance and affectation. . . .

Cowley had more brilliancy of fancy and ingenuity of thought than Donne, with less pathos and sentiment. His mode of illustrating his ideas differs also from Donne's in this : that whereas Donne is contented to analyse an image into its component elements, and resolve it into its most abstracted species; Cowley first does this, indeed, but does not stop till he has fixed upon some other prominent example of the same general class of ideas, and forced them into a metaphorical union, by the medium of the generic definition. Thus he says –

> The Phœnix Pindar is a vast species alone.

He means to say that he stands by himself : he is then 'a vast species alone' : then by applying to this generality the *principium individuationis*, he becomes a Phœnix, because the Phœnix is the only example of a species contained in an individual. Yet this is only a literal or metaphysical coincidence : and literally and metaphysically speaking, Pindar was not a species by himself, but only seemed so by pre-eminence or excellence; that is, from qualities of mind appealing to and absorbing the imagination, and which, therefore, ought to be represented in poetical language, by some other obvious and palpable image exhibiting the same kind or degree of excellence in other things, as when Gray compares him to the Theban eagle,

> Sailing with supreme dominion
> Through the azure deep of air.

Again, he talks in the Motto, or Invocation to his Muse, of 'marching the Muse's Hannibal' into undiscovered regions. That is, he thinks first of being a leader in poetry, and then he im-

mediately, by virtue of this abstraction, becomes a Hannibal;
though no two things can really be more unlike in all the
associations belonging to them, than a leader of armies and a
leader of the tuneful Nine. In like manner, he compares Bacon to
Moses; for in *his* verses extremes are sure to meet. The Hymn to
Light, which forms a perfect contrast to Milton's Invocation to
Light, in the commencement of the third book of *Paradise Lost*,
begins in the following manner : –

> First-born of Chaos, who so fair didst come
> From the old negro's darksome womb!
> Which, when it saw the lovely child,
> The melancholy mass put on kind looks, and smil'd.

And soon after –

> ',Tis, I believe, this archery to show
> That so much cost in colours thou,
> And skill in painting, dost bestow,
> Upon thy ancient arms, the gaudy heav'nly bow.

> Swift as light thoughts their empty career run,
> Thy race is finish'd when begun;
> Let a post-angel start with thee,
> And thou the goal of earth shalt reach as soon as he.

The conceits here are neither wit nor poetry; but a burlesque
upon both, made up of a singular metaphorical jargon, verbal
generalities, and physical analogies. Thus his calling Chaos, or
Darkness, 'the old negro', would do for abuse or jest, but is too remote and degrading for serious poetry, and yet it is meant
for such. The 'old negro' is at best a nickname, and the smile on
its face loses its beauty in such company. The making out the
rainbow to be a species of heraldic painting, and converting an
angel into a post-boy, shew the same rage for comparison; but
such comparisons are as odious as they are unjust.

SOURCE: *Lectures on the Comic Writers – On Cowley,
Butler, Suckling, Etherege, &c.* (1818).

Thomas De Quincey

Omitting Sir Philip Sidney, and omitting his friend, Fulke Greville, Lord Brooke (in whose prose there are some bursts of pathetic eloquence, as there is of rhetoric in his verse, though too often harsh and cloudy), the first very eminent rhetorician in the English literature is Donne. Dr Johnson inconsiderately classes him in company with Cowley, &c., under the title of *Metaphysical* Poets: metaphysical they were not; *Rhetorical* would have been a more accurate designation. In saying *that*, however, we must remind our readers that we revert to the original use of the word *Rhetoric*, as laying the principal stress upon the management of the thoughts, and only a secondary one upon the ornaments of style. Few writers have shown a more extraordinary compass of powers than Donne; for he combined what no other man has ever done – the last sublimation of dialectical subtlety and address with the most impassioned majesty. Massy diamonds compose the very substance of his poem on the Metempsychosis, thoughts and descriptions which have the fervent and gloomy sublimity of Ezekiel or Æschylus, whilst a diamond dust of rhetorical brilliancies is strewed over the whole of his occasional verses and his prose. No criticism was ever more unhappy than that of Dr Johnson's, which denounces all this artifical display as so much perversion of taste. There cannot be a falser thought than this; for, upon that principle, a whole class of compositions might be vicious by conforming to its own ideal. The artifice and machinery of rhetoric furnishes in its degree as legitimate a basis for intellectual pleasures as any other; that the pleasure is of an inferior order, can no more attaint the idea or model of the composition, than it can impeach the excellence of an epigram that is not a tragedy. Every species of composition is to be tried by its own laws; and if Dr Johnson had urged explicitly (what was evidently moving in his thoughts), that a metrical structure, by holding forth the promise of poetry, defrauds the mind of its just expectations, he would have said what is notoriously false. Metre is open to any form of composition, provided it will aid the expression of the thoughts; and the only sound objection to it is, that it has *not* done so. Weak criticism, indeed, is that which condemns a copy of verses under the ideal of poetry, when the mere substitution of another name and classification suffices to evade the sentence, and to reinstate the composition in its rights as rhetoric. It may be very true that the age of Donne gave too much encouragement to his particular vein of composition; that, however, argues no depravity of taste, but a taste erring only in being too limited and exclusive.

SOURCE: 'Rhetoric' (1828).

Ralph Waldo Emerson

I often make the criticism of my friend Herbert's diction that his thought has that heat as actually to fuse the words so that language is wholly flexible in his hands & his rhyme never stops the progress of the sense. And, in general, according to the elevation of the soul will the power over language always be, & lively thoughts will break out into spritely verse. No measure so difficult but will be tractable so that you only get up the temperature of the thought[.] To this point I quote gladly my old gossip Montaigne 'For my part I hold, & Socrates is positive in it, That whoever has in his mind a spritely & clear imagination, he will express it well enough in one kind or another, & tho' he were dumb[,] by signs.'

*

. . . Did I read somewhere lately that the sum of Virtue was to know & dare? The analogy is always perfect between Virtue & genius. One is ethical the other intellectual creation. To create, to create is the proof of a Divine presence. Whoever creates is God, and whatever talents are, if the man create not, the pure efflux of Deity is not his. I read these Donnes & Cowleys & Marvells with the most modern joy; – with a pleasure, I mean, which is in great part caused by the abstraction of all *time* from their verses. What pleases most, is what is next to my Soul; what I also had well nigh thought & said. But for my faith in the oneness of Mind, I should find it necessary to suppose some preestablished harmony, some foresight of souls that were to be & some preparation of stores for their future wants like the fact observed in insects who lay up food before their death for the young grub they shall never see. Here are things just hinted which not one reader in a hundred would take, but which lie so near to the favorite walks of my imagination and to the facts of my experience that I read them with a surprise & delight as if I were finding very good things in a forgotten manuscript of my own.

*

Cowley & Donne are philosophers. To their insight there is no trifle. But philosophy or insight is so much the habit of their minds that they can hardly see as a poet should the beautiful forms & colors of things, as a chemist may be less alive to the picturesque. At the same time their poems like life afford the chance of richest instruction amid frivolous & familiar objects; the loose & the grand, religion & mirth stand in surprising neighborhood and, like the words of great men, without cant.

*

. . . We want soul, soul, soul. A popedom of forms[,] one pulsation of virtue will uplift & vivify. Read Herbert. What Eggs & Ellipses[,] acrostics forward, backward, & across, could not his liquid genius run into, & be genius still & angelic love? And without soul, the freedom of our Unitarianism here becomes cold, barren, & odious[.]

*

. . . It seems a matter of indifference what, & how, & how much, you write, if you write poetry. Poetry makes its own pertinence and a single stanza outweighs a book of prose. One stanza is complete. But one sentence of prose is not.

But it must be poetry[.]

I do not wish to read the verses of a poetic mind but only of a poet. I do not wish to be shown early poems, or any steps of progress. I wish my poet born adult. I do not find youth or age in Shakspeare, Milton, Herbert; & I dread minors.

*

> Herbs gladly cure our flesh because that they
> Find their acquaintance there
> (Herbert, 'Man', 23–4)

This is mystically true. The master can do his great deed[,] the desire of the world, say to find his way between azote & oxygen, detect the secret of the new rock superposition, find the law of the curves, because he has just come out of nature or from being a part of that thing. As if one went into the mesmeric state to find the way of nature in some function & then[,] sharing it[,] came out into the normal state & repeated the trick. He knows the laws of azote because just now he was azote. Man is only a piece of the universe made alive. Man active can do what just now he suffered.

*

What Herbert most excels in is in exciting that feeling which we call the moral sublime. The highest affections are touched by his muse. I know nothing finer than the turn with which his poem on affliction concludes. After complaining to his maker as if too much suffering had been put upon him he threatens that he will quit God's service for the world's :

> Well, I will change the service and go seek
> Some other master out
> Ah, my dear God, though I be clean forgot
> Let me not love thee if I love thee not.

Herbert's Poems are the breathings of a devout soul reading the riddle of the world with a poet's eye but with a saint's affections. Here poetry is turned to its noblest use. The sentiments are so exalted, the thought so wise, the piety so sincere that we cannot read this book without joy that our nature is capable of such emotions and criticism is silent in the exercise of higher faculties.

SOURCE : *Notebooks* (1831–45).

George Macdonald

With a conscience tender as a child's, almost diseased in its tenderness, and a heart loving as a woman's, [Herbert's] intellect is none the less powerful. Its movements are as the sword-play of an alert, poised, well-knit, strong-wristed fencer with the rapier, in which the skill impresses one more than the force, while without the force the skill would be valueless, even hurtful, to its possessor. There is a graceful humour with it occasionally, even in his most serious poems adding much to their charm. . . .

. . . Coming now to speak of his art, let me say something first about his use of homeliest imagery for highest thought. This, I think, is in itself enough to class him with the highest *kind* of poets. If my reader will refer to 'The Elixir', he will see an instance in the third stanza, 'You may look at the glass, or at the sky' : 'You may regard your action only, or that action as the will of God.' Again, let him listen to the pathos and simplicity of this one stanza, from a poem he calls 'The Flower'. He has been in trouble; his times have been evil; he has felt a spiritual old age creeping upon him; but he is once more awake.

> And now in age I bud again,
> After so many deaths I live and write;
> I once more smell the dew and rain,
> And relish versing : O my only light,
> It cannot be
> That I am he
> On whom thy tempests fell all night.

Again:

> Some may dream merrily, but when they wake
> They dress themselves and come to thee.

He has an exquisite feeling of lyrical art. Not only does he keep to one idea in it, but he finishes the poem like a cameo. Here is an instance wherein he outdoes the elaboration of a Norman trouvère; for not merely does each line in each stanza end with the same sound as the corresponding line in every other stanza, but it ends with the very same word. I shall hardly care to defend this if my reader chooses to call it a whim; but I do say that a large degree of the peculiar musical effect of the poem – subservient to the thought, keeping it dimly chiming in the head until it breaks out clear and triumphant like a silver bell in the last – is owing to this use of the same column of words at the line-ends of every stanza. Let him who doubts it, read the poem aloud.

[Quotes 'Aaron'] Note the flow and ebb of the lines of each stanza – from six to eight to ten syllables, and back through eight to six, the number of stanzas corresponding to the number of lines in each; only the poem itself begins with the ebb, and ends with a full spring-flow of energy. Note also the perfect antithesis in their parts between the first and second stanzas, and how the last line of the poem clenches the whole in revealing its idea – that for the sake of which it was written. In a word, note the *unity*....

... It is possible that not many of his readers have observed the following instances of the freakish in his rhyming art, which however result well. When I say so, I would not be supposed to approve of the freak, but only to acknowledge the success of the poet in his immediate intent. They are related to a certain tendency to mechanical contrivance not seldom associated with a love of art: it is art operating in the physical understanding. In the poem called 'Home', every stanza is perfectly finished till the last : in it, with an access of art or artfulness, he destroys the rhyme. I shall not quarrel with my reader if he calls it the latter, and regards it as art run to seed. And yet – and yet – I confess I have a latent liking for the trick. . . .

. . . There can hardly be a doubt that his tendency to unnatural forms was encouraged by the increase of respect to symbol and ceremony shown at this period by some of the external powers of the church – Bishop Laud in particular. Had all, however, who delight in symbols, a power, like George Herbert's, of setting even within the horn-lanterns of the more arbitrary of them, such a light of poetry and devotion that their dull sides vanish in its piercing shine, and we forget the symbol utterly in the truth which it cannot obscure, then indeed our part would be to take and be thankful. . . .

. . . Of Nature's symbols George Herbert has made large use; but he would have been yet a greater poet if he had made a larger use of them still. Then at least we might have got rid of such oddities as the stanzas for steps up to the church-door, the first at the bottom of the page; of the lines shaped into ugly altar-form; and of the absurd Easter wings, made of ever lengthening lines. This would not have been much, I confess, nor the gain by their loss great; but not to mention the larger supply of images graceful with the grace of God, who when he had made them said they were good, it would have led to the further purification of his taste, perhaps even to the casting out of all that could untimely move our mirth; until possibly (for illustration), instead of this lovely stanza, he would have given us even a lovelier :

> Listen, sweet dove, unto my song,
> And spread thy golden wings on me;
> Hatching my tender heart so long,
> Till it get wing, and fly away with thee.

The stanza is indeed lovely, and true and tender and clever as well; yet who can help smiling at the notion of the incubation of the heart-egg, although what the poet means is so good that the smile almost vanishes in a sigh? . . .

. . . I do not know a writer, Wordsworth not excepted who reveals more delight in the visions of Nature than Henry Vaughan. He is a true forerunner of Wordsworth, inasmuch as the latter sets forth with only greater profundity and more art than he, the relations between Nature and Human Nature; while, on the other hand, he is the forerunner as well of some one that must yet do what Wordsworth has left almost unattempted, namely – set forth the sympathy of Nature with the aspirations of the spirit that is born of God, born again, I mean, in the recognition of the child's relation to the Father. Both Herbert and Vaughan have thus read Nature, the latter turning many leaves which few besides have turned. In this he has struck upon a deeper and richer lode than even Wordsworth, although he has not wrought it with half his skill. In any history of the development of the love of the present age for Nature, Vaughan, although I fear his influence would be found to have been small as yet, must be represented as the Phosphor of coming dawn. Beside him, Thomson is cold, artistic, and gray : although larger in scope, he is not to be compared with him in sympathetic sight. It is this insight that makes Vaughan a mystic. He can see one thing everywhere, and all things the same – yet each with a thousand sides that radiate crossing lights, even as the airy particles around us. For him everything is the expression of, and points back to, some fact in the Divine Thought. Along the line of every ray he looks towards its radiating centre – the heart of the Maker.

SOURCE: *England's Antiphon* (1868).

Alexander Grosart

Dr Donne, in a memorable passage, with daring originality, sings of Mrs Drury rapturously :

> Her pure and eloquent soul
> Spoke in her cheeks, and so distinctly wrought,
> That one might almost say her body thought.

I have much the same conception of Crashaw's thinking. It was so emotional as almost always to tremble into feeling. Bare intellect, 'pure' (=naked) thought, you rarely come on in his Poems. The thought issues forth from (in old-fashioned phrase) the heart, and its subtlety is something unearthly even to awfulness. Let the reader give hours to the study of the composition entitled 'In the glorious Epiphanie of ovr Lord God, a Hymn svng as by the three Kings,' and 'In the holy Nativity of ovr Lord God'. Their depth combined with elevation, their grandeur softening into loveliness, their power with pathos, their awe bursting into rapture, their graciousness and lyrical music, their variety and yet unity, will grow in their study. As always, there is a solid substratum of original thought in them; and the thinking, as so often in Crashaw, is surcharged with emotion. If the thought may be likened to fire, the praise, the rapture, the yearning may be likened to flame leaping up from it. . . .

. . . I would have the reader spend willing time, in slowly, meditatively reading the whole of our Poet's sacred Verse, to note how the thinking thus thrills into feeling, and feeling into rapture – the rapture of adoration. It is miraculous how he finds

words wherewith to utter his most subtle and vanishing emotion.
Sometimes there is a daintiness and antique richness of wording
that you can scarcely equal out of the highest of our Poets, or
only in them. Some of his images from Nature are scarcely found
anywhere else. For example, take this very difficult one of ice, in
the Verse-Letter to the Countess of Denbigh, 'persuading' her
no longer to be the victim of her doubts :

> So, when the Year takes cold, we see
> Poor waters *their own prisoners be*;
> *Fetter'd and lock'd fast they lie*
> *In a cold self-captivity.*
> Th' astonish'd Nymphs their Floud's strange fate deplore,
> To find themselves their own severer shoar.

S o u r c e : 'Essay on the Life and Poetry of Crashaw' (1873).

Arthur Symons

. . . Donne's quality of passion is unique in English poetry. It is a rapture in which the mind is supreme, a reasonable rapture, and yet carried to a pitch of actual violence. The words themselves rarely count for much, as they do in Crashaw, for instance, where words turn giddy at the height of their ascension. The words mean things, and it is the things that matter. They can be brutal: 'For God's sake, hold your tongue, and let me love!' as if a long, pre-supposed self-repression gave way suddenly, in an outburst. 'Love, any devil else but you', he begins, in his abrupt leap to the heart of the matter. Or else his exaltation will be grave, tranquil, measureless in assurance.

> All kings, and all their favourites,
> All glory of honours, beauties, wits,
> The sun itself, which makes times, as they pass,
> Is elder by a year, now, than it was
> When thou and I first one another saw.
> All other things to their destruction draw,
> Only our love hath no decay;
> This, no to-morrow hath, nor yesterday,
> Running it never runs from us away
> But truly keeps his first, last, everlasting day.

This lover loves with his whole nature, and so collectedly because reason, in him, is not in conflict with passion, but passion's ally. His senses speak with unparalleled directness, as in those elegies which must remain the model in English of masculine

sensual sobriety. He distinguishes the true end of such loving
in a forcible, characteristically prosaic image :–

> Whoever loves, if he do not propose
> The right true end of love, he's one that goes
> To sea for nothing but to make him sick.

And he exemplifies every motion and the whole pilgrim's progress
of physical love, with a deliberate, triumphant, unluxurious ex-
plicitness which 'leaves no doubt', as we say, 'of his intentions',
and can be no more than referred to passingly in modern pages.
In a series of hate poems, of which I will quote the finest, he
gives expression to a whole region of profound human sentiment
which has never been expressed, out of Catullus, with such in-
tolerable truth.

> When by thy scorn, O murderess, I am dead,
> And that thou think'st thee free
> From all solicitation from me,
> Then shall my ghost come to thy bed,
> And thee, feign'd vestal, in worse arms shall see;
> Then thy sick taper will begin to wink,
> And he, whose thou art then, being tired before
> Will, if thou stir, or pinch to wake him, think
> Thou call'st for more,
> And in false sleep will from thee shrink;
> And then poor aspen wretch, neglected thou
> Bathed in a cold quicksilver sweat wilt lie
> A verier ghost than I;
> What I will say, I will not tell thee now,
> Lest that preserve thee; and since my love is spent
> I'had rather thou should'st painfully repent,
> Than by my threatenings rest still innocent.

Yet it is the same lover, and very evidently the same, who win-
nows all this earthly passion to a fine, fruitful dust, fit to make

bread for angels. Ecstatic reason, passion justifying its intoxica-
tion by revealing the mysteries that it has come thus to apprehend, speak in the quintessence of Donne's verse with an
exalted simplicity which seems to make a new language for love.
It is the simplicity of a perfectly abstract geometrical problem,
solved by one to whom the rapture of solution is the blossoming
of pure reason. Read the poem called 'The Ecstasy', which seems
to anticipate a metaphysical Blake; it is all close reasoning, step
by step, and yet is what its title claims for it.

It may be, though I doubt it, that other poets who have
written personal verse in English, have known as much of
women's hearts and the senses of men, and the interchanges of
passionate intercourse between man and woman; but, partly by
reason of this very method of saying things, no one has ever
rendered so exactly, and with such elaborate subtlety, every
mood of the actual passion. It has been done in prose; may one
not think of Stendhal, for a certain way he has of turning the
whole forces of the mind upon those emotions and sensations
which are mostly left to the heat of an unreflective excitement?
Donne, as he suffers all the colds and fevers of love, is as much
the sufferer and the physician of his disease as we have seen him
to be in cases of actual physical sickness. Always detached from
himself, even when he is most helplessly the slave of circumstances, he has that frightful faculty of seeing through his own
illusions; of having no illusions to the mind, only to the senses.
Other poets, with more wisdom towards poetry, give us the
beautiful or pathetic results of no matter what creeping or soar-
ing passions. Donne, making a new thing certainly, if not always
a thing of beauty, tells us exactly what a man really feels as he
makes love to a woman, as he sits beside her husband at table, as
he dreams of her in absence, as he scorns himself for loving her, as
he hates or despises her for loving him, as he realises all that is
stupid in her devotion, and all that is animal in his. 'Nature's lay

idiot, I taught thee to love', he tells her, in a burst of angry contempt, priding himself on his superior craft in the art. And his devotions to her are exquisite, appealing to what is most responsive in woman, beyond those of tenderer poets. A woman cares most for the lover who understands her best, and is least taken in by what it is the method of her tradition to feign. So wearily conscious that she is not the abstract angel of her pretence and of her adorers, she will go far in sheer thankfulness to the man who can see so straight into her heart as to have

> Found something like a heart,
> But colours it and corners had;
> It was not good, it was not bad,
> It was entire to none, and few had part.

Donne shows women themselves, in delight, anger, or despair; they know that he finds nothing in the world more interesting, and they much more than forgave him for all the ill he says of them. If women most conscious of their sex were ever to read Donne, they would say, He was a great lover; he understood.

And, in the poems of divine love, there is the same quality of mental emotion as in the poems of human love. Donne adores God reasonably, knowing why he adores him. He renders thanks point by point, celebrates the heavenly perfections with metaphysical precision, and is no vaguer with God than with woman. Donne knew what he believed and why he believed, and is carried into no heat or mist as he tells over the recording rosary of his devotions. His 'Holy Sonnets' are a kind of argument with God; they tell over, and discuss, and resolve, such perplexities of faith and reason as would really occur to a speculative brain like this. Thought crowds in upon thought, in these tightly-packed lines, which rarely admit a splendour of this kind : –

> At the round earth's imagined corners, blow
> Your trumpets, angels, and arise, arise
> From death, you numberless infinities
> Of souls, and to your scattered bodies go.

More typical is this too knotted beginning of another sonnet : –

> Batter my heart, three person'd God ; for, you
> As yet but knock, breathe, shine, and seek to mend ;
> That I may rise, and stand, o'erthrow me, and bend
> Your force, to break, blow, burn, and make me new.

Having something very minute and very exact to say, he hates to leave anything out; dreading diffuseness, as he dreads the tame sweetness of an easy melody, he will use only the smallest possible number of words to render his thought; and so, as here, he is too often ingenious rather than felicitous, forgetting that to the poet poetry comes first, and all the rest afterwards.

For the writing of great poetry something more is needed than to be a poet and to have great occasions. Donne was a poet, and he had the passions and the passionate adventures, in body and mind, which make the material for poetry; he was sincere to himself in expressing what he really felt under the burden of strong emotion and sharp sensation. Almost every poem that he wrote is written on a genuine inspiration, a genuine personal inspiration, but most of his poems seem to have been written before that personal inspiration has had time to fuse itself with the poetic inspiration. It is always useful to remember Wordsworth's phrase of 'emotion recollected in tranquility', for nothing so well defines that moment of crystallisation in which direct emotion or sensation deviates exquisitely into art. Donne is intent on the passion itself, the thought, the reality; so intent that he is not at the same time, in that half unconscious way which is the way of the really great poet, equally intent on the form, that both may come to ripeness together. Again it is the heresy of the realist.

Just as he drags into his verse words that have had no time to take colour from men's association of them with beauty, so he puts his 'naked thinking heart' into verse as if he were setting forth an argument. He gives us the real thing, as he would have been proud to assure us. But poetry will have nothing to do with real things, until it has translated them into a diviner world. That world may be as closely the pattern of ours as the worlds which Dante saw in hell and purgatory; the language of the poet may be as close to the language of daily speech as the supreme poetic language of Dante. But the personal or human reality and the imaginative or divine reality must be perfectly interfused, or the art will be at fault. Donne is too proud to abandon himself to his own inspiration, to his inspiration as a poet; he would be something more than a voice for deeper yet speechless powers; he would make poetry speak straight. Well, poetry will not speak straight, in the way Donne wished it to, and under the goading that his restless intellect gave it.

He forgot beauty, preferring to it every form of truth, and beauty has revenged itself upon him, glittering miraculously out of many lines in which he wrote humbly, and leaving the darkness of a retreating shadow upon great spaces in which a confident intellect was conscious of shining.

> For, though mind be the heaven, where love may sit,
> Beauty a convenient type may be to figure it.

he writes, in the 'Valediction to his Book', thus giving formal expression to his heresy. 'The greatest wit, though not the best poet of our nation', Dryden called him; the greatest intellect, that is, which had expressed itself in poetry. Dryden himself was not always careful to distinguish between what material was fit and what unfit for verse; so that we can now enjoy his masterly prose with more equable pleasure than his verse. But he saw clearly enough the distinction in Donne between intellect and the poetical spirit; that fatal division of two forces, which, had they pulled together instead of apart, might have achieved a result wholly splendid. Without a great intellect no man was ever a great poet; but to possess a great intellect is not even a first step in the direction of becoming a poet at all.

Compare Donne, for instance, with Herrick. Herrick has little enough of the intellect, the passion, the weight and the magnificence of Donne; but, setting out with so much less to carry, he certainly gets first to the goal, and partly by running always in the right direction. The most limited poet in the language, he is the surest. He knows the airs that weave themselves into songs, as he knows the flowers that twine best into garlands. Words come to him in an order which no one will ever alter, and no one will ever forget. Whether they come easily or not is no matter; he knows when they have come right, and they always come right before he lets them go. But Donne is only occasionally sure of his words as airs; he sets them doggedly to work of saying something, whether or no they step to the beat of the music. Conscious writer though he was, I suppose he was more or less unconscious of his extraordinary felicities, more conscious probably of how they came than of what they were doing. And they come chiefly through a sudden heightening of mood, which brings with it a clearer and a more exalted mode of speech, in its merely accurate expression of itself. Even then I cannot imagine him quite reconciled to beauty, at least actually doing homage to it, but rather as one who receives a gift by the way.

SOURCE: *Fortnightly Review* (1899).

T. S. Eliot

It is difficult to find any precise use of metaphor, simile, or other conceit, which is common to all the poets and at the same time important enough as an element of style to isolate these poets as a group. Donne, and often Cowley, employ a device which is sometimes considered characteristically 'metaphysical'; the elaboration (contrasted with the condensation) of a figure of speech to the furthest stage to which ingenuity can carry it. Thus Cowley develops the commonplace comparison of the world to a chess-board through long stanzas 'To Destiny', and Donne, with more grace, in 'A Valediction', the comparison of two lovers to a pair of compasses. But elsewhere we find, instead of the mere explication of the content of a comparison, a development by rapid association of thought which requires considerable agility on the part of the reader.

> On a round ball
> A workeman that hath copies by, can lay
> An Europe, Afrique, and an Asia,
> And quickly make that, which was nothing, *All*,
> So doth each teare,
> Which thee doth weare,
> A globe, yea world by that impression grow,
> Till thy tears mixt with mine doe overflow
> This world, by waters sent from thee, my heaven dissolved so.

Here we find at least two connexions which are not implicit in the first figure, but are forced upon it by the poet: from the geographer's globe to the tear, and the tear to the deluge. On the other hand, some of Donne's most successful and characteristic effects are secured by brief words and sudden contrasts :

> A bracelet of bright hair about the bone,

where the most powerful effect is produced by the sudden contrast of associations of 'bright hair' and of 'bone'. This telescoping of images and multiplied associations is characteristic of the phrase of some of the dramatists of the period which Donne knew : not to mention Shakespeare, it is frequent in Middleton, Webster, and Tourneur, and is one of the sources of the vitality of their language. . . .

. . . It is certain that the dramatic verse of the later Elizabethan and early Jacobean poets expresses a degree of development of sensibility which is not found in any of the prose, good as it often is. If we except Marlowe, a man of prodigious intelligence, these dramatists were directly or indirectly (it is at least a tenable theory) affected by Montaigne. Even if we except also Jonson and Chapman, these two were notably erudite, and were notably men who incorporated their erudition into their sensibility : their mode of feeling was directly and freshly altered by their reading and thought. In Chapman especially there is a direct sensuous apprehension of thought, or a recreation of thought into feeling, which is exactly what we find in Donne :

> in this one thing, all the discipline
> Of manners and of manhood is contained;
> A man to join himself with th' Universe
> In his main sway, and make in all things fit
> One with that All, and go on, round as it;
> Not plucking from the whole his wretched part,
> And into straits, or into nought revert,
> Wishing the complete Universe might be
> Subject to such a rag of it as he;
> But to consider great Necessity.

We compare this with some modern passage :

> No, when the fight begins within himself,
> A man's worth something. God stoops o'er his head,
> Satan looks up between his feet – both tug –
> He's left, himself, i' the middle; the soul wakes
> And grows. Prolong that battle through his life !

It is perhaps somewhat less fair, though very tempting (as both poets are concerned with the perpetuation of love by offspring), to compare with the stanzas already quoted from Lord Herbert's Ode the following from Tennyson :

> One walked between his wife and child,
> With measured footfall firm and mild,
> And now and then he gravely smiled.
>   The prudent partner of his blood
>   Leaned on him, faithful, gentle, good,
>   Wearing the rose of womanhood.
> And in their double love secure,
> The little maiden walked demure,
> Pacing with downward eyelids pure.
>   These three made unity so sweet,
>   My frozen heart began to beat,
>   Remembering its ancient heat.

The difference is not a simple difference of degree between poets. It is something which had happened to the mind of England between the time of Donne or Lord Herbert of Cherbury and the time of Tennyson and Browning; it is the difference between the intellectual poet and the reflective poet. Tennyson and Browning are poets, and they think; but they do not feel their thought as immediately as the odour of a rose. A thought to Donne was an experience; it modified his sensibility. When a poet's mind is perfectly equipped for its work, it is constantly amalgamating disparate experience; the ordinary man's experience is chaotic, irregular, fragmentary. The latter falls in love, or reads Spinoza, and these two experiences have nothing to do with each other, or with the noise of the typewriter or the smell of cooking; in the mind of the poet these experiences are always forming new wholes.

We may express the difference by the following theory: The poets of the seventeenth century, the successors of the dramatists of the sixteenth, possessed a mechanism of sensibility which could devour any kind of experience. They are simple, artificial, difficult, or fantastic, as their predecessors were; no less nor more that Dante, Guido Cavalcanti, Guinicelli, or Cino. In the seventeenth century a dissociation of sensibility set in, from which we have never recovered; and this dissociation, as is natural, was aggravated by the influence of the two most powerful poets of the century, Milton and Dryden. Each of these men performed certain poetic functions so magnificently well that the magnitude of the effect concealed the absence of others. The language went on and in some respects improved; the best verse of Collins, Gray, Johnson, and even Goldsmith satisfies some of our fastidious demands better than that of Donne or Marvell or King. But while the language became more refined, the feeling became more crude. The feeling, the sensibility, expressed in the 'Country Churchyard' (to say nothing of Tennyson and Browning) is cruder than that in the 'Coy Mistress'.

The second effect of the influence of Milton and Dryden followed from the first, and was therefore slow in manifestation. The sentimental age began early in the eighteenth century, and continued. The poets revolted against the ratiocinative, the descriptive; they thought and felt by fits, unbalanced; they reflected. In one or two passages of Shelley's *Triumph of Life* in the second *Hyperion*, there are traces of a struggle toward unification of sensibility. But Keats and Shelley died, and Tennyson and Browning ruminated.

After this brief exposition of a theory – too brief, perhaps, to carry conviction – we may ask, what would have been the fate of the 'metaphysical' had the current of poetry descended in a direct line from them, as it descended in a direct line to them? They would not, certainly, be classified as metaphysical. The possible interests of a poet are unlimited; the more intelligent he is the better; the more intelligent he is the more likely that he will have interests: our only condition is that he turn them into poetry, and not merely meditate on them poetically. A philosophical theory which has entered into poetry is established, for its truth or falsity in one sense ceases to matter, and its truth in another sense is proved. The poets in question have, like other poets, various faults. But they were, at best, engaged in the task of trying to find the verbal equivalent for states of mind and feeling. And this means both that they are more mature, and that they wear better, than later poets of certainly not less literary ability.

SOURCE : 'The Metaphysical Poets' (1921).

PART THREE
Recent Studies

Rosemond Tuve

THE CRITERION OF DECORUM (1947)

I. DECORUM AND 'LITERARY' DICTION

There is little evidence that, to either the sixteenth or the seventeenth century, poetic decorum involved cutting out some images because they were not suitable 'to poetry', or putting in others because of some intrinsic 'literary' elegance or charm. When a mere handbook-writer like Sherry gives a list of 'ungarnished' figures, and we look at them expecting to find ways of using language that are too commonplace for literature, we find them distinguished as indecorous not because they are insufficiently high-flown, but because words and subject are unsuited. 'Bomphiologia' uses gay and blazing words for a light matter; 'asiatismus' is a kind of inditing full of figures but lacking in matter; there are various other classifications of language too much befigured and begayed, (fols ix ff. [1555]). Or, as in the vices of incongruity distinguished by Fabri (1521), the fault is sometimes lack of economy or significancy.[1] Puttenham mocks at one of these, in an image; quoting six lines on spring, complete with Dan Phoebus's rays and Aries's horned head, he remarks that 'the whole matter is not worth all this solemne circumstance to describe the tenth day of March'.

These exemplify the common position on 'poetic diction'. Precisely what is damned is (1) the gaudy and (2) the inane. The

principle invoked to damn them is that of decorum. Quite probably we should not admire certain single examples of decorously
elaborate figures which these gentlemen would have considered
properly outside the nets they spread for the indecorous. But at
all events what their definitions of decorum attempt is to snare
the very creature sometimes thought of as encouraged to enter
under that heading – 'literary' elegance. Writers in this era do
not talk about a style suitable to poetry; they talk about many
poetic styles suitable to many poetic subjects. The emphasis is
consistently that in Fracastoro's unequivocal statement concerning the language of the poet, who alone speaks *simpliciter*:

But when I speak of simply beautiful language I wish to be understood in this way : that this beauty harmonizes with the subject
under discussion and is appropriate to it and its different attributes,
and is not merely beautiful in and for itself [*Naugerius*, p. 64, trans.
of fol. 160ʳ (1555)].

As a robe of gold does not dignify a peasant, he says, so heroic
dignity given to a light subject is unseemly. Perhaps one of our
real quarrels with the Renaissance lies in our evaluation of
peasants and of heroic dignity; perhaps new judgements as to
which *are* weighty matters and which inconsequential, were
forming even as early as the sixteenth century. This is not primarily a difference in poetic.

When we examine actual examples of phrases condemned by
sixteenth-century writers as indecorous, we do frequently find
that their preferred phrases seem like 'poetic diction' to us on just
this score – that we are quite willing to lower some subject which
they thought fit to heighten. Puttenham objects to a translation
of Virgil which says that Aeneas was fain to *trudge* out of Troy;
this were better spoken of a beggar, a rogue, or a lackey; 'for so
wee use to say to such maner of people, be trudging hence'. A
historiographer does not write of a king or emperor that he took

to his heels and ran out of the field, though of a mean soldier or captain this 'were not undecently spoken'. Juno must not *tug* at Aeneas; it is a carter's word and connotes the pulling of oxen and horses, or boys tugging each other by the ear. Perhaps we forget that usages or 'decencies' which happen to fit within our own sense of values do not, like these, seem like arbitrary elevation of language, but like what these really are – an attempt to fit the word to the idea we have of the object. Daily readers of the *New York Times* would expect it to say that John L. Lewis *ramped* up and down the room, that his beetle-brows pushed his two small sharp eyes together like a greedy mole's – but not to say the same of Einstein. The latter image might conceivably be used to mark an ironic contrast between Einstein's outer man and his meaning to the world of thought; but, if so, heightened language would inescapably accompany the exalting *of the latter*. We, too, do what Peacham says is decent and due – bow the knee of our speech and light up the eye of our phrase to the bright beams of earthly glory. When Puttenham boggles at a translator's calling Aeneas a *fugitive*, seeing in this 'a notable indignity offred to that princely person', his *grounds* are impeccable : first, that the connotations of words are important and powerful and, second, that it is 'not to the Authours intent', *he meant not to make him a fugitive.*

The grounds for Elizabethan insistence upon decorum have often been assumed, rather, to be a certain reverence for poetic etiquette, trivially defined, and for 'literary' diction, in and for itself. This sort of mistranslation of the underlying motive of various critical strictures has had unfortunate effects in the history of criticism.

II. DECORUM AND THE LOWERING OF STYLE

Even more important misinterpretations of the concept of
decorum have resulted from another habitual oversight, still very
common. Most examples above happen to be instances of decorum working toward elevation of style. This is only half the
story. Decorum worked quite as consistently toward lowering the
style to suit the author's subject and intent. Modern remarks
about decorum seldom show an appreciation of this side of the
matter. There is plenty of room in orthodox theory for what we
like to think of as audacious images, or for the poem which uses
images as one of the most economical of all elements in poetic
technique for deflating rather than inflating the importance,
value or prestige of something.

Puttenham happens to exemplify outright this double operation of decorum by an image which is indecorous used for one
subject, decorous when used for another, precisely because it has
this deflating effect, in the second instance desirable. The word
used, *pelf*, has by now all but lost its metaphorical sense, so that
to us the question is not one of imagery; to Puttenham *pelf* is
still 'properly the scrappes or shreds of taylors and of skinners,
which are accompted of so vile price as they be commonly cast out
of dores'. He reprimands a poet for saying, in a verse in dis-
praise of a rich man : '*thou hast a princes pelfe*'. This, he says,
is 'a lewde terme to be spoken of a princes treasure'.[2] But what
is interesting is his defense of the decorum of the belittling image
pelf in *case* the poetic subject requires this diminution. In the
image condemned, this metaphor

carrieth not the like reason or decencie, as when we say in reproch of
a niggard or userer . . . . that he setteth more by *a little pelfe* of the
world, than by his credit or health, or conscience. For in comparison
of these treasours, all the gold or silver in the world may by a skorne-

full terme be called pelfe, & *so ye see that the reason of the decencie holdeth not alike in both cases.*

This is sound poetic, and a clear and plain exemplification of the tenet that decorum *demands in the proper situations* homely, displeasing, harsh images – which are poetic, not 'unpoetic', *because* they have that character. Incidentally, it illuminates very considerably the reasons for the use of such images by the Metaphysicals.

It can properly be claimed for the Metaphysical poets, I think, that exactly this kind of keeping poetic decorum, when 'abbasing a matter', is responsible for most of their rough or homely images – ironic and self-depreciating, unpleasing, or just surprisingly down-to-earth. They may make unorthodox evaluations of men and things; I find little that is unorthodox in this respect about their images or their poetic. At least I can find few if any 'low' images which can be questioned as out of line with the accepted requirements of decorum, in Donne, King, Carew, Suckling, Marvell, the Herberts.[3] Certainly not in the mystical poets, for their type of subject and intention had required from time immemorial this magnification of the *in*significance of things which other men accepted as significant and desirable (this is what the 'pelf' image does to the gold and silver).

I find, of course, a great many contributory reasons for the *predominance* of 'deflating' images in the verse of these poets: the genres in which their best work was done (an extremely narrow list compared with that of the 1590s); the development of reflective 'lyric' forms written in the base or middle styles; changed intentions attendant on the separation of some forms from music; the growing importance of prose as a vehicle for graver matters which in previous centuries had been treated in verse (as Suckling and Lord Herbert, for example, left us treatises rather than poems 'of religion' and 'of truth'); many factors affecting single poets – such as the fact that many of these poets have left us little work done in their mature years, or the fact that if the Donne who wrote the sermons had put all his ideas into poems he might have had a somewhat different set of advocates in the 1930s. In general, reasons underlying what we like to think of as the peculiar character of Metaphysical imagery are far too complicated to obey our desire to force them into some simple generalization about pessimism or psychological conflict. It is tempting but inaccurate to see in these poets a reflection of our own need to defy hierarchical principles like that of fitness and proportion.

Donne is peculiarly sensitive to what the keeping of decorum required of his imagery. The exact propriety of his images is perhaps the largest factor in the vigor and acuteness of his style, for the poet has no sharper instrument than this, especially if he be in other ways a deft logician. Of all elements in poetic technique it is most economical, and relative brevity was required in all the kinds Donne chose to write in. Unless he chooses to have his images convey two evaluations at once (which he can do with unambiguous skill, generally subscribing to but one), he is particularly adept at seizing on images in which the thrust is lightning-quick and unmistakable in direction.

With short images, this is often because they are familiar or make use of some known convention. If Donne wishes to shrink up the world and its sun into nothing, beside the marvellous greatness of God brought to the incredible paradox of a human death, then we have :

> What a death were it then to see God dye? . . . .
> It made his footstoole crack, and the Sunne winke.
>
> ('Goodfriday, 1613')

Both of these last are unassailably decorous images. Their fitness is traditional; men had not waited for the Copernican theory to point – at the moment of the Crucifixion – to the inglorious littleness of man's world. The rhetoric of the whole passage, with its interwoven echoes of *death–die–life*, and the rush of the repeated grammatical structures, helps to give the images their effect of shocking disintegration. If Donne wishes rather to stretch the world's diameter out to unimaginable distances, then we have, instead of this cracked stool,

> At the round earths imagin'd corners, blow
> Your trumpets, Angells, and arise, arise. . . . .
>
> ('Holy Sonnets', vii)

It is not possible to separate the images from the metrical pattern in which they inhere, and the bold sponde and triumphant upspringing rhythm underline the extension of earth's limits rapidly denoted through the remaking of the doubly familiar image (*round, corners*).

Donne is already on his way to another amplification : 'arise arise / From death, you numberlesse infinities / Of soules . . . '. A very different crowd, though it is precisely the same one, from that in the resurrection-image of 'The Relique', where his intention is rather to diminish the importance of these innumerable millions. There, he is amplifying instead a love which outlasts all earthly events, and to which even the Day of Resurrection offers pre-eminently a last lovers' meeting :

> Who thought that this device might be some way
> To make their soules, at the last busie day,
> Meet at his grave, and make a little stay . . .

The indecorous and truly dissonant image would put this busy rush of other souls intent on their own destinations into the serious grandeur of the sonnet; or put the trumpeting Gabriel up onto the mere footstool; or point to the world's splendor and the sun's unceasing march in lines on the death of that Son who begot for men a different kind of endless day.[4]

It is necessary, if we would stay with orthodox theory, to rid ourselves of the notion that some images are inherently decorous, likewise of the notion that the 'trivial' or superficially inelegant image is indecorous. Like Puttenham, we must examine the final purport of the image in connection with the poem's 'cause'.[5] In poems where Donne scoffs at the notion that ' ''Tis not the bodies marry, but the mindes', he is ready to swear that women 'are but *Mummy*, possest' ('Loves Alchymie'); in poems arguing that 'Chang'd loves are but chang'd sorts of meat' he will conclude: 'And when hee hath the kernell eate, / Who doth not fling away the shell?' ('Communitie'). These diminishings, or bitter reductions into low and common terms, are entirely decorous for a poet with such a subject and purpose in hand. They would not be decorous, and do not appear, in poems whose subject is the parting of lovers 'Inter-assured of the mind', or which treat 'Loves mysteries [which] in soules doe grow'. Then we have rather love's enduring strength *amplified* through 'Like gold to ayery thinnesse beate', or exposition of the relation between body and essential self through an elevated cosmological similitude.[6]

All these differences are simply examples of what Puttenham is driving at when he points out 'that the reason of the decencie holdeth not alike in both cases'.

There are occasional examples of violent diminishing figures which I at least am unable to defend on grounds of decorum, and it might be useful to point out one or two. In the 'Elegie on M^{ris} Boulstred', Donne's first two lines show how consciously he used language to amplify or diminish[7] a subject:

> Death I recant, and say, unsaid by mee
> What ere hath slip'd, that *might diminish thee.*

Two lines later he begins a long amplification of Death's power, harshly reducing the earth and all things on it to the miserable dimensions they take on in respect of this power : 'Th' earths face is but thy Table; there are set / Plants, cattell, men, dishes for Death to eate. / In a rude hunger now hee millions drawes / Into his bloody, or plaguy, or sterv'd jawes.' These images, for twenty lines, are violent and horrible – but a heightened awareness of Death's power is scarcely an indecorum in an elegy (first section). The image that seems to me indecorous by the poetic of the time occurs as Donne proceeds to claim that M^ris Boulstred is one of those few who are but made God's own by dying, Death's blow being so ineffective :

> She was more stories high : hopeless to come
> To her Soule, thou 'hast offer'd at her lower roome.

The wrench by which we are made to conceive of the relation between soul-and-body, higher-and-lower, in purely spatial terms, seems to me out of keeping with what the rest of the poem tries to say about that relationship. It is not the vehicle used in the comparison which makes it disproportionate; a following image is decorous enough :

> As houses fall not, though the King remove,
> Bodies of Saints rest for their soules above.

The flaw seems to be in the logic; a frivolous *libertin* poem might expound through images the subject 'our souls are just our top stories', but this poem gives no other indication of such an intention.

I relegate a second example to the notes,[8] but in both, and contrary to his usual practice, Donne seems to do what we expect of Symbolist poets – admit as an image a kind of isolated fancy which arose, largely by association, out of his original notion ('overthrowing' in the first, 'death th' Ocean' in the second). But, in any case, the first poem especially runs from interest to interest somewhat too gaspingly.

It is natural enough that these examples come from Donne's *Epicedes* and *Obsequies*. Their images have come in for much abuse, frequently from objectors who take for granted a connection between intellectual ingenuity and insincerity. Defenders of Donne deny the connection, but frequently by providing us with a substitute scapegoat – other poets' rhetorical ingenuity, seen as a vice. Decorum as understood in this period bears out neither kind of ingenuity in poems of deep feeling. Possession of either may no more be our touchstone for the integrity of images than may the use of inelegant or unpleasant vehicles of comparison. All the epicedes miss the sweeping power and profundity of the *Anniversaries*. Yet the images in these last are certainly no less ingenious. The first, the 'Anatomie', is occupied with one long metaphor used to diminish, a method quite in accord with the poem's stated subject – 'the frailty and the decay of this whole World'. The violent single examples of diminishing – the world a carcass, a cripple, a wan ghost, a dry cinder – are strictly proportioned to the nature of the subject.

I have used Donne to exemplify normal and accepted ways in which decorum operated to lower rather than to elevate a subject through images, because it was expedient to use the work of a single poet and because so much has been made of his harsh, violent, or displeasing images. It seems to me an error to call these images dissonant or audaciously discordant. They are not inharmonious with the subjects he chose, not do I think that his half-century saw them so; they are sometimes inharmonious with a given reader's preconceived notion of what kind of subject the contemplation of 'Love' or 'Woman' or 'The Soul' *ought to* lead one to propound. Donne's subjects are audacious and so is his unabashed importation of the strictness of logic into the poetic genres he preferred. But we use amplifying images to commend, diminishing images to condemn, every day of our lives; such a use of imagery implies no daring new tenet in the poetic of its user. These ugly or homely images are for the most part simply the ordinary rhetorical figure meiosis, recommended by the orthodox rhetorician for just the purposes for which the Metaphysical poets (and the others) used it.

Puttenham calls this figure the Disabler. It may be used 'in derision and for a kind of contempt', as in some of the examples above from Donne: the used woman a shell to fling away, the sun eclipsed with a wink, men as mere dishes for Death. It comes into play 'if you diminish and abbase a thing by way of spight or malice, as it were to deprave it', as in 'A heavy burthen perdy, as a pound of fethers' (Puttenham). The figure meiosis is not new to our discussion; it is simply the type of amplification which is decorous if one intends appraisal which lessens rather than magnifies. Hoskins says that *diminution* differs from amplification 'no otherwise than up-hill and down-hill'. One may make impressive the smallness of a man's wisdom by saying, *he is not the wisest man that ever I saw*. In one of its meanings it is thus simply litotes. And, as Hoskins remarks, 'why should I give examples of the most usual phrases in the English tongue?'

However, in this form of litotes and in certain others it takes, meiosis happens to be peculiarly useful for poets when they wish – often because they are condemning or complaining – by indirection to seek direction out. There are certain innocent-looking uses of the figure 'by way of pleasant familiaritie' – as Puttenham says, he may call his Muse *my moppe*, 'a litle prety Lady, or tender young thing'. Such uses, however, may range from endearing diminutives to more serious and dignified diminutions which get a troublesome thing into manageable dimensions, seen as its true ones. This sort occurs in Herrick's remark to his tiresome conscience: 'Can I not sin, but thou wilt be / My private Protonotarie?' Or in Herbert's, to his: 'Peace pratler, do not lowre'. Or in Southwell's advice to lovers to leave off the idle pain of serving love 'delightful in the rind, / Corrupted in the core' ('Love's servile lot'). These simpler diminutions, which enable a poet to indicate by an image his sense of the true proportions of a thing, are to be distinguished from disabling images which carry a faint tinge of the author's disbelief that these are necessarily the true dimensions of the thing. The simpler use does not have, for example, the disappointed bitterness of Donne's 'women . . . . are but *Mummy*, possest' (i.e., would they *were* thus easily dismissed, once had). Or the sardonic tone of Eliot's 'Am an attendant lord, one that will do / To swell a progress, start a scene or two' ('Prufrock').

The difference lies in the presence or absence of *ironia*, a figure frequently accompanying or superimposed upon meiosis. If it is present, the author does not wholeheartedly subscribe to the diminishing. We can judge of irony only in a context, as we must depend upon inferences regarding the poet's other and real meaning. For example, we could not tell except for Puttenham's *comment* whether the line calling a burden no heavier than a pound of feathers was said by a man cheering the bearer up ('heavy, but you can take it') or seeing truth under appearance ('nonsense, mere feathers'). *Ironia* is not present in the second.

It should be clear, then, that 'diminishing' may be either ironic or not ironic. The irony may be slight, a mere denying of the contrary (litotes). Then, as Hoskins says, this figure 'sometimes in ironious sort goes for amplification' – we may mean that a personage is great and call him 'no mean man'. We simply intend to be taken as saying a mere modicum of what we mean. The irony may be simple, a mere affirming of the contrary, when we quite clearly do not mean what we say. Thus Donne will say that he does not believe it possible to find a woman both true and fair, by telling us to effect a string of impossibilities which he does not mean us even to attempt. That a hypothetical such she might last until we write our letter is not litotes; it is overstatement. All such images are meiosis using irony of a fairly simple sort.

The irony may be more complicated. The poet may mean not so much what he appears to say as something else, unmentioned. Hoskins gives as examples of diminutions, from Sidney:

Those fantastical-minded people which children and musicians call lovers.

This color of mine, which she in the deceivable style of affection would entitle beautiful.

The first is not the considered opinion even of Musidorus; he yet means enough of it to intend it as a dash of the cold water of fact upon Pyrocles's flame. Meiosis has commonly this tempering or astringent effect. When a poet himself dashes cold water on his own fervency, or fervency he thinks others may attribute to him, then we have the kind of irony which has in recent years all but usurped the entire definition of the term. There is an element of this self-conscious and somewhat youthful self-protectiveness in the second example. 'Do not think I do not correctly estimate my own limitations', says Pyrocles's meiosis in the second quotation. When the ironic reservation is a more important one, or is maturely seen and faced as one of those tormenting doubts which universally prick men's confidence in the validity of cherished truths, then the irony appears rather as a courageous and thoughtful willingness to see all aspects of reality.[9]

Both in its derisive and in its ironic form, meiosis is obviously a figure of marked usefulness in all writing with a satiric intent and is therein particularly pleasing for its decorousness. It is also naturally useful in reflective poetry, the more as this is argumentative in tone or approaches dialectic in method and intention. The form in which irony embodies an 'objection foreseen' is peculiarly natural to the method of dialectic, since a first requirement of the

method is that the contrary of a position, later refuted, must be
stated with authoritative power, or, in poetry, with utmost vividness. A powerful ironic figure of extreme logical subtlety will in
effect convey the two contradictory positions on some question
which it is the business of the whole poem's dialectic to resolve.
More frequently, figures are flatly opposed to each other in
the manner of the *débat*. It is revealing to see Marvell break
down a problem into opposed but still ironic figures in debates
like those between soul and body or soul and pleasure, with the
help of the prosopopoeia he has chosen as a structure. He will
counter one meiosis with another, and in each case the nature of
this figure operates as a criticism of the opposing position, so that
we obtain from the whole the impression of a peculiarly honest
and inclusive consideration. Again, this is not new. The dialogue
of Daniel's *Musophilus* exemplifies the same process, though the
wit of the radical or homely figure impresses less because of
differences in length and in metrical form and skill. Ironic and
superficially 'indecorous' images in Spenser's Mutability Cantos
are evidence of a similar intention; despite the necessities imposed by the epic form (on tempo and pace especially), the
rough insolence of some of the images and the insinuating
quality of others reveal the normal effect of meiosis, in this
earliest important attempt to state seriously in poetry the
accusations later so common in *libertin* thought.

But it is wiser to exemplify from shorter poems. We detect
(through the violence of the paradox) that Marvell does not
entirely assent to the enslaved Soul's 'diminishings' of those
capabilities which make the body 'for sin so fit' :

> Here blinded with an Eye; and there
> Deaf with the drumming of an Ear.
> A Soul hung up, as 'twere, in Chains
> Of Nerves, and Arteries, and Veins.
>   ('A Dialogue between the Soul and Body')

Yet, also, in the Body's remarks about 'this ill Spirit', the tyrannic Soul, we feel the poet's own ironic qualifications – a dry reminder, in the figure's hyperbolical inconsequence, that only the Body would think being upright is responsible for falling:

> Which, stretcht upright, impales me so,
> That mine own Precipice I go;
> And warms and moves this needless Frame;
> (A Fever could but do the same.)

In this poem Marvell introduces no 'Chorus' to indicate his resolution of the question, and I do not think that it is possible to know the extent of the irony in the concluding figure:

> What but a Soul could have the wit
> To build me up for Sin so fit?
> So Architects do square and hew,
> Green Trees that in the Forest grew.

Throughout the poem the Body rebels against capacities which it has by virtue of being informed with Soul; the architect image would thence presumably be read as another of the Body's impatient objections to the discipline of Form. If one wishes to erect it into something more than this (into a statement of Marvell's rebellious preference for the 'natural' and unspoiled, for example), one must do it upon indecisive grounds like the poet's other uses of the connotations of *green*; or one may be tempted by 'The Mower against Gardens' to apply Rousseauistic notions in interpreting the images of an era which in general quite approved of what the art of the architect necessitated doing to the green trees.[10] The Body stands by its own answer convicted of a sophistry if we weight the irony heavily, that is, if we think of Marvell as taking a critical rather than a naïve attitude toward the logical flaw in the Body's argument. A readiness to listen to the notion that 'he who perfects trees into buildings is part author of the ill uses they are put to' characterizes a later era

than Marvell's; perhaps the ambiguity is not so much in
the poem as imposed by understandings we bring to it. But this
is to some extent unavoidable with tropes, and the images remain
partially ambiguous, much as though Marvell had juxtaposed
in a single dialectical poem the values emphasized in 'The
Garden' and in 'To his Coy Mistress.' Ironic figures demand
more frequently than any others this admission that we cannot
be sure, from the images alone, what the poet meant. The Metaphysical poets knew this as well as or better than we; hence they
commonly buttress such figures with statement.

It is perhaps worth while to distinguish one other function of
meiosis, not usually ironic, which is more common in hortatory
writing and in lyrics which persuade, plead, or justify. Puttenham says that the figure can be used as a 'kind of Extenuation
when we take in hand to comfort or cheare any perillous enterprise, making a great matter seem small, and of litle difficultie'.
Since, as Peacham says, it often serves to plant hope or to ex-
cuse, all writers of love poems (including the Metaphysicals)
find use for it in complaints or protestations. Suckling cheers himself as the sonnet writers had done with calling attention to 'how
unregarded now / That *piece* of beauty passes'. Carew in
'Eternity of love protested' puts lesser lovers into the low category of 'paper set on fire'. Obviously, such figures are useful only
in certain types of poetic situation; neither the poets nor we ourselves reach out for belittling images when our design is to
praise, a fact which may be swiftly substantiated in Herrick,
Shakespeare, Donne, Spenser or Yeats. A lover protesting
against ill usage, however, is likely to put proud ladies in their
place with a meiosis. One who is justifying an uncomplimentary
estimate will make the matter small with a violent diminuition :

> As a bathtub lined with white porcelain,
> When the hot water gives out or goes tepid,

So is the slow cooling of our chivalrous passion,
O my much praised but-not-altogether-satisfactory lady.
(Ezra Pound, 'The Bath Tub', from *Lustra* [1915])

This is a common type of image in daily speech, falls in with the simple derisive use of meiosis to undervalue that which no longer seems desirable, and is everywhere met with. Drayton tells 'His Rivall' that 'she to thee / Reades *but old Lessons over*' (II, 369); Daniel reminds his lady that 'Men doe not weigh *the stalke* for that it was, / When once they finde her flowre, her glory passe' (*Delia*, xxxii). Lodge tells his that though her skin is soft like wool of wethers, she exhibits 'Solemn vows, but sorry thinking'; and, since 'Others warm them *at my fuel*', he concludes by advising himself: 'Change *thy pasture*, take thy pleasure'. Lodge's 'fuel' diminishes the fire of love into a sort of stolen household coal; Donne can amplify it by the use of the very same noun :

Make her for love fit fewell. . . . .
So may shee faire, rich, glad, and in nothing lame,
To day put on perfection, and a womans name.
('Epithal. made at Lincolnes Inne' [Author's italics])

These are *not* 'the same image'; they differ because purpose and surroundings change the way words are understood, change our evaluation of what they refer to. To call both 'radical images' points to a characteristic, but not a distinguishing characteristic. Neither is more or less decorous, more or less daring, more or less dissonant, than the other.

All these images are decorous. They suit the cause and purpose that the author has in hand. A disbeliever in love should speak like a disbeliever in love; there is a reason in Nature for it. It is true that we feel a twinge of rebellion when Whetstone comes out flat with 'grave olde men should instruct', 'Clownes should speake disorderlye'. But he places his reason squarely in

the nature of things, and we are forced to agree that in so far as
they *are* grave or clownish, so they will speak, and that this is
truly what enables a writer to 'worke a Comedie *kindly*' – according to men's natures (Dedication to *Promos and Cassandra*
[1578]). We read poetry on the understanding that a poet will
not 'use one order of speach for all persons' – e.g., for those
different persons: himself as sardonic commentator, himself as
serious reasoner, himself as ardent lover. When poets do, and
we protest that their poems are vapid in tone, insensitive and un-
discriminating in the use of images, pretentious and unreal in
their attempt to convey thoughts and emotions, our protest is
really Whetstone's own – that they have committed 'a grose
Indecorum, for a Crowe wyll yll counterfet the Nightingale's
sweete voice'. Many a Whetstone remained for all his pains a
crow, yet the fault lay not in the notion of what should be done
but in the difficulty of the doing.

Similarly, warnings against indecorous diction or imagery
which may seem to us rigid curbs on the poet's freedom are
seldom truly such because they do not ignore or deny this fundamental conception of the relation of imagery to purpose.[11]
Hoskins merely states a law of communication to which most
poets try to conform, and the workings of which all readers
experience daily, when he warns: 'But ever (*unless your purpose
be to disgrace*) let the word be taken from a thing of equal or
greater dignity'. There are nevertheless infinite variations
within this purpose of 'disgracing', and, moreover, the poet's
skill in part controls the 'dignity' of the things (as in Donne's
fit fewell).

Except for this warning that words are headstrong, that their
connotations may throttle one's intentions in a poem, the
principle of decorum calls little attention to the area whence content of comparisons is drawn. Attention is centred on the cogency
and illuminating power of the relation between two terms;

if this outshines the stubborn irrelevancies present *in every comparison*, then the image is decorous. On such considerations depend the defenses which we find of the radical and the far-fetched image. They are praised because they surprise the attention into alertness and because they give a more vigorous intellectual pleasure – both modern grounds as well. They are not defended on the modern ground that, when one of the terms is of a low imaginative value, the achievement of the poet in making such links gives the verse higher imaginative intensity. In earlier theory attention is directed toward the intrinsic imaginative value of the terms only in so far as a habitual value may play havoc with, or enhance, their relatableness. The poet's task is to bring out those possibilities of relation which are pertinent to his purpose and veil those which are not. In this he is not merely the user, but the creator, of language.

Suggestions, like denotative meanings, are judged pleasing for their fit relation rather than assumed to be pleasant for some imaginative quality they inherently possess. Connotations which have nothing to do with the poem seem not to be prized whether they are 'imaginative' or not – that is, suggestion is thought of as controlled, whether tending towards amplification or diminution, and strictures such as those I have quoted warn the poet that there are cases where words can escape his control. Hence Puttenham refers the determination of decorum to the *judgment*.[12] He finds an infinite variety of reasons why poets will find infinitely varied images to be fitting, but he leaves no doubt as to which faculty must finally help the poet to decide whether they are so :

it resteth in the discerning part of the minde, so as he who can make the best and most differences of things by reasonable and wittie distinction is to be the fittest iudge or sentencer of [*decencie*], (Author's italics.)

The poet is thus given great freedom, though subject always to the discipline of his own alert judgment. He may seize his comparable terms from wherever he wishes, provided he can wittily detect, and make impressive, similitudes missed by others, with that peculiar acuteness for seeing relations which Aristotle praises in the *Poetics*. What he must not do is to blunder into connotations which are unwanted: 'if ye abase your thing or matter by ignorance or errour in the choise of your word', you have not the subtle ironic reservation or controlled suggestion of meiosis, but the vice of tapinosis (Puttenham).[13] 'Bomphiologia', the opposite vice, is just as bad. A radical, homely image is a tapinosis if its diminishing connotations are unwanted, confusing, or unmanageable; a pleasingly decorative image is a 'bomphiologia' if it distorts. Otherwise one type of image is as decorous as the other.

Modern criticism of Elizabethan and Metaphysical writing neither recognizes that the radical image was orthodox in early literary theory nor admits the necessity of this degree of rational control.

Unlike a modern post-Symbolist critic, when Hoskins expressly praises the radical image, he praises not the poet's awareness and reconciliation of diversities but his perception of a forceful similarity; the diversities in the terms, far from being pleasurable for introducing subtle overtones of meaning, are neglected, meant not to obtrude themselves. The entire emphasis is upon the agreements which the poet reveals – once the wit of the comparison has achieved that initial surprise which makes the 'amplification' more 'forcible' (the *amplification*, not the possible ironic qualifications of it). These agreements truly exist, to be seen by any discerning mind; they obtain logically, are discovered, not conjectured, are pleasing because they are so apt, not because they are so wretched.[14] It seems to me that such an understanding of the witty forcefulness of the radical image should be urged as the typical Metaphysical understanding of it. Better than the modern understanding (which is bent on revealing a kind of tortured confusion in these poets), it fits the rest of what they put in their poems, the matrix in which such images are imbedded.

Donne particularly shows as a surer artist and a clearer and more mature thinker if we read his innumerable vivid diminishing images and subtle but firm ironic figures by the light of these traditional understandings. One cannot but perceive the delicacy and needle-like acuteness with which he can convey overtones in cases where the rest of the poem shows that he clearly intended to do so. Hence it seems to me illegitimate to fit out his poems with overtones which diverge ambiguously from his apparent meaning and which are only to be traced in the connotations of his image terms. This method of attributing meaning to Metaphysical poems should be restricted to those whose knowledge of Elizabethan linguistic habits far outshines that of a mere *NED*. It seems illegitimate, for example, to conjecture that Donne's choice of a compass (in order to illuminate how 'our two soules' be one) has some equivocal force used of lovers, or was meant to cast an obscure ironic shadow. It is to us rather than to Donne that compasses are part of the commonplace paraphernalia of high-school mathematics.[15] Donne is so adept at conveying intended ironic reservations that I find it more reasonable to believe that he did not intend us, for example, to attend to suggestions of the numerous ridiculous differences between souls and bullets, while he wittily distinguishes (in *the trajectory of* the two) three quite dignified logical likenesses :

> And so my soule more earnestly releas'd,
> Will outstrip hers; As bullets flowen before
> A latter bullet may o'rtake, the pouder being more.
>
> ('The Dissolution')

Much of the supposed rebellious 'indecorum' of homely or radical Metaphysical images disappears when we thus observe every caution not to read what was not written. Reading what the poet did not write is, of course, entirely allowable as a way of enjoying poems (is even inevitable because of the nature of tropes, but there are safeguards). It is only that findings resulting from this pursuit should not creep into our critical judgments of the poet's aims or a period's character. Such findings are part of literary history – but of the history of the *critic's* period.

S O U R C E : *Elizabethan and Metaphysical Imagery* (1947).

NOTES

1. 'Pleonasmus' and 'macrologia' add superfluous words, 'perittologia' uses words without pith, 'periergia' uses many words for a small matter. Puttenham names the last 'overlabour' 'for his overmuch curiositie and studie to shew himself fine in a light matter', and exemplifies it (p. 258) as below. Day (1595), treating such figures, implies that if seeming superfluity increases our reasons (i.e., underscores our intentions), it is permissible.

2. Of course, this notion is easier to smile at now than in 1589. It is only fair to quote from Puttenham's earlier chapter : 'for neither is all that may be written of Kings and Princes such as ought to keepe a high stile, nor all that may be written upon a shepheard to keepe the low, but according to the matter reported' (chap. v).

3. The demonstrations of decorous single images which follow are all subject to revision when we shall have new knowledge about the exact connotations of particular words to Elizabethans and Jacobeans. Much of the required knowledge is forever inaccessible to us. The type of linguistic research necessary before we shall be able to pronounce with real sureness on what was 'indecorous' in specific images is exemplified in A. H. King's *Languages of Satirical Characters in 'Poetaster'* (London, 1941).

4. Donne can amplify what is conventionally amplified when he chooses. The sun may be used to signify might and power, or may find its traditional use to figure forth the greatness of a king : 'The

Sun it selfe, *which makes times,* as the passe' ('The Anniversarie');
'A Taper of his Torch, a copie writ / From his Originall, and a
faire beame / Of the same warme, and dazeling Sun . . .' ('To Sir
H. W. at his going Ambassador to Venice'). But naturally this is not
what he does when he wishes rather to amplify the power of something beside which the sun's greatness becomes a mere external
irrelevance : '*Busie old foole,* unruly Sunne, ... Thy beames, so
reverend, and strong / Why shouldst thou think? / I could eclipse
and cloud them with a winke, / But that I would not lose her sight
so long' ('The Sunne Rising').

5. I . . . use this untranslatable Elizabethan term because it
combines the meanings of 'poetic subject' and 'poet's intention' so
economically. Although close to the Aristotelean 'final cause', it has,
as used by Elizabethans, less of self-conscious calculation than our
words 'aim' or 'purpose'. 'Subject' is open to confusion with 'subject
matter', and in both Latin and English critical treatises 'subject'
and related words (*object, subjective reality*) are troublesome to
translate, retaining implications taken on through scholastic usage
even, evidently, as late as Descartes.

6. E.g., 'Our bodies why doe wee forbeare? / They are ours,
though they are not wee, Wee are / The intelligences, they the
spheare' ('The Extasie'). I do not disregard claims that the subject
of this poem is almost opposite to that I have stated (in the semi-
quotation from vs. 71-2), but consider these claims to have been
sufficiently answered. For the controversy, see G. R. Potter, 'Donne's
"Extasie", Contra Legouis', *Philological Quarterly*, xv (1936) 247–53,
and references. The other poem used above is 'A Valediction : forbidding mourning'.

7. I use 'amplify' somewhat inaccurately and untechnically
here; all diminishing is a form of amplification – magnifying the
lack of power, dignity, or value of something. I should also remark
that in a swift review of many images it is not possible to state
subjects of poems with anything like a proper subtlety or inclusive-
ness. That is done by the poem.

8. Cf. the 'Elegie on the Lady Marckham', v. 17 : 'In her this
sea of death hath made no breach, / But as the tide doth wash the
slimie beach, / And leaves embroder'd workes upon the sand, / So
is her flesh refin'd by deaths cold hand.' 'Slimie' is a fairly usual

word for the body, not too harsh to be decorous, for instance, in
Spenser's Castle of Alma, where a paradoxical contrast *is* pointed
at, between the substantial impermanence and goodly workmanship
of man's body (*Faerie Queene*, ii, ix, 21). But here it magnifies
disproportionately (for me) the lowness of flesh which in a line or
so is said to have been 'Diamonds, Rubies, Saphires, Pearles',
especially when an image denoting change (not decoration) of
substance was really wanted. That the image seems both trivial and
violent may be because I cannot abstract as quickly as Donne's
contemporaries could, and have less interest in what happens to my
flesh after death.

9. The difference could be exemplified by two of Donne's uses
of meiosis to make ironic reference to a problem. In the somewhat
youthfully self-concerned 'Love Alchymie', the question of where
love's 'centrique happinesse doth lie' receives vivid metaphorical
statement, and the diminishing figures are harsh and contemptuous,
although I believe also ironic, e.g. : 'Our ease, our thrift, our honor,
and our day, / Shall we, for *this vaine Bubles shadow* pay?' In
'The Canonization' there is more of cogent argument, and instead
of begging the question he moves from the meiosis in the line '*Call
her one, mee another flye*', to the sequent amplifications which lead
him into the center of his subject : 'We 'are Tapers too . . . . And wee
in us finde *the 'Eagle and the Dove*. /The *Phoenix* ridle hath more
wit / By us. . . . .' The figure quoted from 'Prufrock' a few paragraphs
above ('Am an attendant lord . . . .') is this last type of rather
complicated ironic meiosis.

10. The complex of ideas is a very different one in 'The Mower',
where man's arrogant seizing of an illegitimate sovereignty over
Nature is in question. As usual in the Renaissance, the artificial is
not condemned in itself but with respect to its motivation; artifice
is 'allow'd' to 'Man, that sov'raign thing', but not perverted artifice,
dealing in 'Forbidden mixtures'.

11. Even when Hoskins warns against using metaphors that are
'too base' (e.g., *shoulders of friendship*, or *a red herring is a shoeing-
horn to a pot of ale*), he yet concludes, 'But they that speak of a
scornful thing *speak* grossly'.

12. Although he admits the complexity and variety of judgments
on whether this or that speech 'be decent or indecent' and notes

the importance of much observation and experience of how language works as a social phenomenon.

13. Peacham exemplifies it; if you want dignity, do not call the Thames a *brook*, or a 'foughten field' a *fray*. 'Bomphiologia', conversely, gives high praises to small deserts.

14. Of course, Renaissance theory has room also for the profound symbol (not usually 'far-fetched') of wider and deeper import. But concerning the type here discussed, see Hoskins's paragraph on 'Policy is like the sea'; also his praise of 'great affinity' if 'different' things are compared. The sixteenth century was entirely aware of what Dr Johnson was to notice; 'And you shall most of all profit by inventing [finding] matter of agreement in things most unlike, as London and a tennis court : for *in both all the gain goes to the hazard*'. [Author's italics.]

15. At all events, in 1608 the court audience could be trusted to interpret both the zodiac and the compass as 'known ensignes of *perfection*'; see Jonson's *Masque of Beautie* (gloss; author's italics), and on the whole approach to imagery here exemplified see the book on *The Symbolic Persons in the Masques of Jonson* by A. H. Gilbert, to whom I owe this reference (Durham, N.C., forthcoming). See Plate 36*f*, in D. J. Gordon, 'The Imagery of Ben Jonson's *The Masque of Blacknesse* and *The Masque of Beautie*', *Journal of Warburg and Courtauld Institutes*, vi (1943) 122–41.

Leo Spitzer

'THE EXTASIE' (1949)

John Donne's poem 'The Extasie' (published in 1633) begins
by describing the outward situation of two lovers, reclining on a
grassy, violet-scented mound near a river bank; against this background they experience mystic union of a Neo-Platonic order,
without being diverted or disturbed by physical passion.

> Where, like a pillow on a bed,
>   A pregnant banke swel'd up, to rest
> The violets reclining head,
>   Sat we two, one anothers best.
> Our hands were firmely cimented   5
>   With a fast balme, which thence did spring,
> Our eye-beames twisted, and did thred
>   Our eyes, upon one double string;
> So to'entergraft our hands, as yet
>   Was all the meanes to make us one,   10
> And pictures in our eyes to get
>   Was all our propagation.
> As 'twixt two equall Armies, Fate
>   Suspends uncertaine victorie,
> Our soules, (which to advance their state,   15
>   Were gone out,) hung 'twixt her, and mee.
> And whil'st our soules negotiate there,
>   Wee like sepulchrall statues lay;
> All day, the same our postures were,
>   And wee said nothing, all the day.   20
> If any, so by love refin'd,

That he soules language understood,
And by good love were growen all minde,
    Within convenient distance stood,
He (though he knew not which soule spake,   25
    Because both meant, both spake the same)
Might thence a new concoction take,
    And part farre purer then he came.
This Extasie doth unperplex
    (We said) and tell us what we love,   30
Wee see by this, it was not sexe,
    Wee see, we saw not what did move :
But as all severall soules containe
    Mixtures of things, they know not what,
Love, these mixt soules, doth mixe againe,   35
    And make both one, each this and that.
A single violet transplant,
    The strength, the colour, and the size,
(All which before was poore, and scant,)
    Redoubles still, and multiplies.   40
When love, with one another so
    Interinanimates two soules,
That abler soule, which thence doth flow,
    Defects of lonelinesse controules.
Wee then, who are this new soule, know,   45
    Of what we are compos'd, and made,
For, th'Atomies of which we grow,
    Are soules, whom no change can invade.
But O alas so long so farre
    Our bodies why doe wee forbeare?   50
They are ours, though they are not wee, Wee are
    The intelligences, they the spheare.
We owe them thankes, because they thus,
    Did us, to us, at first convay,
Yeelded their forces, sense, to us,   55
    Nor are drosse to us, but allay.
On man heavens influence workes not so,
    But that it first imprints the ayre,
Soe soule into the soule may flow,

Though it to body first repaire.   60
As our blood labours to beget
  Spirits, as like soules as it can,
Because such fingers need to knit
  That subtile knot, which makes us man :
So must pure lovers soules descend   65
  T'affections, and to faculties,
Which sense may reach and apprehend,
  Else a great Prince in prison lies.
To'our bodies turne wee then, that so
  Weake men on love reveal'd may looke;   70
Loves mysteries in soules doe grow,
  But yet the body is his booke.
And if some lover, such as wee,
  Have heard this dialogue of one,
Let him still marke us, he shall see   75
  Small change, when we'are to bodies gone.

The author evidently intends to offer, in poetic guise, an intellectual definition of the ecstatic state of two souls, which emerge
from their bodies and blend so completely that they become one.
The Greek term *ekstasis*, 'going forth', is literally paraphrased in
line 15 : 'Our soules, (which to advance their state, were *gone
out*,)', a line which must be contrasted with the final one :
'Small change, when we'are *to bodies gone*'; i.e., when we return to unecstatic normal life. Two phenomena must be described
by the poet : the separation of soul from body (the *ekstasis*
proper) and the union of the two souls. Both are explained by
a technique of insisting and re-insisting on the same facts which
are described with a wealth of variations. I shall list first the
varied references to the idea : 'two become one' :

    4   we two one anothers best
    5   our hands were firmely cimented
    8   thred our eyes upon one double string
 9–10   to entergraft our hands, . . . to make us one

15–16   our soules . . . hung 'twixt her and mee
26   both meant, both spake the same
35   (love these) mixt soules (doth mixe againe)
36   makes both one, each this and that
41–2   [love] with one another . . . interinanimates
        [= animates] two soules
59   soule into the soule may flow
74   this dialogue of one

The concept of 'union' suggests the corollary idea of 'pro-creation'; and, indeed in our poem, we shall find references to the fruit of the lovers' union – which must be on the same spiritual plane as the union itself :

5–6   [our hands were firmely cimented] with a
        fast balme, which *thence did spring*
11–12   [pictures . . . was all our] propagation
15   our soules, (which to *advance their state*
        were gone out)
27   [he who would be a witness to our union]
        thence a new concoction [= distillate, state
        of maturation] take
43   that *abler* soule, which thence doth flow
45   wee, then, who are *this new soule*

And we may add further the first two lines: 'Where, like a pillow on a bed, / A Pregnant banke swel'd up', which give to the intellectual procreation of the lovers a background of exuberantly fertile nature and vegetative life;[1] this passage should be taken together with ll. 37–40 (though this quatrain may strike us as a later interpolation): just as a single violet, transplanted into new soil, thrives with renewed life, so the single souls, offered a new soil by love (the soil of two-ness), will 'redouble and multiply' their potentialities.

As for the idea of the ecstasy proper, this is taken up in the simile (ll. 13–17) of the two armies between which Fate hangs

and for which the souls negotiate – a simile which is carried over
into the following image of a double tombstone with recumbent
figures from which the souls have fled. Again the idea of the un-
embodied souls recurs in line 22 '('by good love . . . growen all
minde') and in ll. 47–8 : 'For th'Atomies of which we grow, /
Are soules, whom no change can invade'; 'We [our soules] are /
The intelligences, they [our bodies] the spheare' (in medieval cosmology the spheres are moved by the angelic intelligences).

The last third of the poem is entirely given over to a justification of the body : since this must be abandoned if the soul would
know ecstasy, one might assume that the body is only a hindrance
for the spirit. And yet Donne insists on rehabilitating the body,
describing the service it renders the spirit. By means of the
senses the body mediates between the affianced souls : the body
is not 'drosse', but 'allay' (l. 56). Moreover, it produces the
blood-spirits (*spiritelli, esprits vitaux*) which are closely knit to
the soul and produce those sensuous images that lead toward the
revelation of love : 'Loves mysteries in soules doe grow, / But
yet the body is his booke.' Donne ends by repeating the motif of
the changelessness of souls that have once united in ecstasy.

We cannot escape the impression that the poet proceeds in
the whole poem in the manner of a believer who has, firmly
established in his mind, a conception of which he wishes to convince his audience. Indeed, so conscious is he of the need to *convince* others that, not content with the audience of his readers,
he would introduce (l. 21) into the poem itself, 'within con-
venient distance' of the lovers, a witness, or a listener, able to
understand the language of love, who would listen to the 'dialogue of one' (l. 73). Such a one, he assures us, could not but
testify both to the purity of the mystic act and to the lasting effect
of ecstasy, even after the return of the ecstatic souls to the
bodies.

As for his audience of readers, the technique the poet adopts

in order to convince us, is a quantitative one: he must multiply
his evidence in order to hammer home his conviction. With ever-
new similes (*to ciment, to graft, balm, concoction, to string,
violet*), or with new coinages (*entergraft, interinanimate*) he
forges the idea 'two become one', and with accumulation of
similes (negotiators for armies, sepulchral figures, intelligences
not spheres, alloy not dross, mystery not book) the idea of
ecstasy is given form. This revelation itself is portrayed from an
intellectual point of view, as the paradoxical mathematical re-
duction: '2 becomes 1'. The depth of the mystic experience, the
feeling of its ever-increasing depth, is not expressed: nothing is
revealed of the genesis of this experience, of the development up
to the culminating moment of trance. The ecstasy has existed from
the beginning: it is clearly named 'this Extasie' in line 29: it
lasts not a moment, but the whole day through. We are allowed
to share only the enduring state of bliss-without-desire. Statu-
esque calm prevails throughout the poem. We see before us an
allegorical statue of Ecstasis which stands unveiled from the beginning, while the flexible figures of speech circle about it,
weaving ethereal wreaths around it, casting ever-new shadows
upon it – a composite allegorical figure indeed, of which are pre-
dicated attributes belonging to different realms of life. To express
the same observation by varying the well-known couplet of
Robert Frost:

> They all dance around in a circle and suppose,
> But the *concept* sits in the middle, and knows.

All the sciences and crafts are allowed to enter our poem in the
form of metaphors and to testify to the central concept: the craft
of the perfumer, of the jeweller who strings pearls, of the
gardener who transplants, of the military negotiator, of the
sculptor, of the alchemist who distills 'concoctions', of the cos-
mologist who deals with the atomic structure of the universe –

they all parade before the statue in a pageant, a Petrarchian *triumphus pudicitiae.*

Connected with Donne's quantitative procedure is his use of hyperbole, often misunderstood by the critics: he tells us that so great was the ecstasy, that (ll. 7–8) 'Our eye-beames twisted, and did thred / Our eyes, upon one double string' – a feat none too easily visualized. But he means, of course, to predicate the impossible. According to the requirements of metaphysical wit, he must ascribe to what he praises the physically impossible as well as the limitless: not only must he marshal all the kaleidoscopic richness of the earth, he must introduce the unvisualizable possibilities of the impossible – well aware that with all his effort his panegyric must, in the end, still be an approximation. Of course, this type of eulogy has the effect of distancing the object of praise: Donne does not re-enact what is within him, but points us to something above him. Instead of the re-creation of the intuitive experience the poet actually had, with its particular quality, we are offered an encyclopedic, discursive analysis. Yet this is informed by rhythmic beauty: the beauty of the rhythm of simple spoken speech with all its convincingness – a rhythm that echoes the inner event and testifies to the veracity of the report. Notice the rhythm (indicating 'sameness' by chiastic 'return to the same'), which accompanies the simile of the 'sepulchre' (ll. 18–20):

> We like sepulchrall statues lay;
> *All day,* the same our postures were,
> And wee said nothing, *all the day.*

The rhythm by which the 'new soul' is portrayed as beyond change (ll. 45–8):

> Wee, then, who are this new soule, know,
> Of what we are compos'd, and made,

> For, th'Atomies of which we grow,
> Are soules, *whom no change can invade.*

or the meditative rhythm of the lines that indicate the non-sexual nature of that love (ll. 31–2) :

> *Wee see* by this, it was not sexe,
> *Wee see, we saw* not what did move. . . .

It can be no chance that the rhythm chosen by the poet is most convincing where the immutability of the union is contrasted with transient phenomena. After having noted that in our poem the intellectual kernel of an intuitive state of mind has been made concrete and that an experience which must have developed in time has been reduced to timelessness, we may observe that the last part, that in which the justification of the body is offered (love begins in the body and will continue when the souls have returned to the body), is poetically less successful than the rest – and this, in spite of occasional poetic gems, such as (l. 64) 'That subtile knot, which makes us man' (a line which turns the succinct definition of the psycho-physical nature of man into poetry), or (l. 68) 'Else a great Prince in prison lies', where for one moment we seem to see the Segismundo of Calderon in his tower, deprived of the light of his senses. The final part of the poem verges on a scientific treatise of physiology, that is, of seventeenth-century physiology. Any reader must feel here a poetic anti-climax (he may even suspect composition of that last part at a different time) : after we have known of the ecstasy of two souls become one, the idea of their return or 'descent' to that body is disconcerting. For mortal man is so constituted that he can visualize a state of bliss only as an apex that must stand out in isolation, a death within life followed by silence; Goethe's Egmont exclaims : 'Let me die, the world has no joy greater than this', and the curtain must fall.

Donne, however, wished to make the ecstatic vision tributary to
the daily life which must follow – and which could be enhanced
by the remembrance thereof. But this very noble moral thought,
so deeply connected with religious reformation and regeneration,
has not come to poetic fruition; for, after having shared an
ecstasy which is beyond time and change, we are not ready to
return to the world where change, however slight, is possible.
And the repetition of the motif of the witness who would observe
the lovers in their post-ecstatic life is an indication that here
Donne's poetic imagination was lagging.

Moreover, we feel somehow that Donne himself, in spite of
his endeavor to justify the flesh was more intimately convinced of the reality and beauty of the spiritual union than of
the necessity of the body for that union. It may well be that the
basically Protestant mind of Donne is responsible for this self-
contradictory attitude. For estrangement from the body may be
said to be characteristic of Protestantism, whereas in the Jewish
faith the rights of the body can easily coexist with the claims of
the Creator on man's immortal soul, and, in the Catholic
religion, a bridge from soul to body is afforded by the church
sacrament according to which Christ is present in the bodily
union of the believers, who are *membra Christi.* In the
Protestant monument erected by Donne to the mystic union, the
figures impersonating this union show the touch of a firmer hand
than does the pedestal of clay by which he would have them sup-
ported. Donne knows, in fact, no true answer to that tormenting
question: 'But O alas, so long, so farre / Our bodies why doe
wee forbeare?' It is no chance that the word 'sex' (l. 31) is used
in our poem for the first time in European literature in the
modern sense of the specific, objective, definable, but questionable, urge that conditions the life of man and woman. Again in
his poem 'The Primrose' Donne says: '. . . should she / Be more
then woman, shee would get above / All thought of sexe . . .'; to

'get above all thought of sexe' goes hand in hand with 'Wee see by this, it was not sexe' : in both cases, 'sex' is treated as a lesser factor which exists to be transcended.

However, if sex is envisaged (so sharply!) as a thing to be dismissed, we can, of course, not expect to find in Donne a representative of religious mysticism, which (as we know from Evelyn Underhill's studies on mystical psychology) borrows from sex the raw material of psycho-physical sensitivity with which to welcome, on a higher plane, *but still in one's body* as well as in one's soul, the invasion of the divine.

It is the Spanish mystics who, in their procedure of giving flesh to spiritual experience (while sharing Donne's ultimate attitude of disillusion, *desengaño*, toward the body), have found the most direct way to reconcile the splendor of the body, rediscovered by the Renaissance, and the supernatural beauty of divine grace, experienced in medieval meditation. And yet, our poem, with its clear demarcation between body and soul, will remain a monument of intellectual clarity. How characteristic is the verb 'unperplex' (l. 29) which Donne has coined (and allowed to rhyme with 'sex' – a counterbalance!), how revelatory of Donne's passionate desire for intellectual clarification of emotions! And it is this urge which has made John Donne so dear to our age, an age sore perplexed, mistrusting instinctual emotion – preferring, perhaps, clarity of analysis to syntheses which it can no longer wholeheartedly ratify.

In view of the interpretation I have suggested for Donne's poem, it is hardly necessary to state that I am utterly opposed to the opinion offered by the late Professor Legouis in his *Historie de la littérature anglaise*. Legouis, who evidently has in mind the numerous poems in which Donne has ridiculed the theme of Platonic love (think of 'The Flea'!), sees in our poem a 'sophistical' and 'insidious' plea for physical consummation. The two lovers, after having enjoyed for a full day the sensation of having formed one soul,

sentent qu'ils sont devenus de purs esprits. De la hauteur où ils planent, que le corps est peu de chose! Pauvre corps, mais qui pourtant mérite sa récompense pour les avoir menés l'un vers l'autre. Il n'est que juste de penser à lui! 'Pourquoi s'abstiennent nos corps si longtemps? . . . Sans cela un grand prince gît en prison.'

Now, in order to justify such a carnal interpretation, Legouis has interpreted line 50 ('Our bodies why doe wee forbeare?') as if 'forbear' meant, not 'endure, tolerate', as I have understood it, but 'restrain, control' ('pourquoi s'abstiennent nos corps si long-temps?'). Furthermore, in the last line: 'Small change, when we'are to bodies gone', which I have explained as referring to the inevitable return from ecstasy to every-day life, he evidently sees an allusion to physical love. And what we have taken as a description of the beginning of love (which must start with the body), as a point from which to reach the ecstasy – he assumes to constitute an invitation, *hic et nunc*, to indulge the body; and the noble line 68: 'Else a great Prince in prison lies', descriptive of the mortal condition of man, he brings in, somehow, as the climax of the carnal invitation: the individual man's eternal self-pitying plea to the woman.

Before such Gallic worldly wisdom, such familiarity with the age-old stratagems of a resourceful seducer (of a Valmont in the *Liaisons Dangereuses*), how naïve my own earnest remarks may appear! It sometimes happens, however, that candor is the most direct way of understanding; I have chosen simply to believe the poet when he speaks, at the beginning, with the unmistakable voice of truth, of the beauty, and reality, of the spiritual ekstasis: and if we do believe him here, we can not, then, see in the last part an invitation to carnality – which could only mean that the first part was a mere stratagem. And the lines with their sincere and final ring, 'Wee see by this, it was not sexe, / Wee see, we saw not what did move' – is this the tone of hypocrisy? We should suspect that the speaker knew at the time that sex *did* move (or would move)? And that witness upon whom Donne calls at the end, 'When we'are to bodies gone' – incredible to think that Donne is calling upon him to witness the physical act : he whom the poet has described as 'by good love . . . growen all minde' (notice the lofty Augustinian phrase *good love = amor bonus*)!

No, I still prefer to see in our poem a glorification of true ekstasis (lacking perhaps in artistic convincingness, for the noble reason earlier suggested) rather than a circuitous exhibition of lofty Neo-Platonic philosophy destined only to bring about the inevitable earthy dénouement : I see in it not an *argumentum ad hominem*, or rather . . . *ad feminam*, but, in accord with Donne himself, a 'dialogue of one' – of, if you wish, a monologue of two.

SOURCE: *A Method of Interpreting Literature* (1949).

NOTE

1. The 'pregnant banke swel'd up to rest the violets reclining head' is obviously a feature belonging to the literary 'ideal landscape', a *topos* recently treated by E. R. Curtius, *Europäische Literatur und lateinisches Mittelalter* (Bern, 1948) p. 196 et seq.; the ultimate sources are such passages as Virgil, *Bucolics* III, 55–7 :

Dicite, quandoquidem *in molli consedimus herba,*
Et nunc omnis ager, nunc omnis *parturit* arbos;
Nunc frondent silvae; nunc formosissimus annus.

This is exactly the *décor* to be found in Donne's poem : a spot in nature, made beautiful by exuberant vegetation, inviting repose and enjoyment. In another ideal landscape of Virgil (*Buc.* II, 45 et seq.), we find eight species of flowers mentioned and with the late Roman poet Tiberianus, four (among them also the violets : 'tum nemus fragrabat omne violarum spiritu'); Donne, however, mentions only the violet, probably because he wished to emphasize the climate of love, for, with the ancients, the violet is the flower symbolic of love : 'tinctus viola pallor amantium' (Horace, *Odes* III, 10) : 'palleat omnis amans, hic est color aptus amanti' (Ovid, *Ars amatoria* I, 729). Cf. in Petrarch 'S'un *pallor di viola e d'amor* tinto', '*Amorosette* e *pallide viole*' (*Concordanze delle Rime di Fr. Petrarca*, ed. McKenzie, s.v. *viola*); in Camoens 'Pintando estava alí Zéfiro e Flora/*As violas da côr dos amadores*' (*Lusiads* IX, 61 ; cf. Richard F. Burton, 'Camoens', II, 657).

S. L. Bethell

THE NATURE OF METAPHYSICAL WIT (1953)

I

A few years ago enthusiasts for 'metaphysical' poetry usually said of it that it possessed 'sensuous immediacy', that it was composed by the method of 'thinking in imagery', and that it aimed not at stating universal truth but at expressing a precise 'definition of emotion' or 'experience' or 'states of mind' in particular situations. When philosophical notions were employed by the poet, it was with no regard for their truth or falsity but with the sole purpose of illustrating and clarifying this 'definition'. Those who were not enthusiasts for metaphysical poetry were, I think, merely unhelpful, and, although the phrases in inverted commas above now start a blush in the critical cheek, I fear I have at one time and another been guilty of them all. Two things, however, I could never believe: first, that Donne was indifferent to the truth of the philosophical propositions he employed, and – much more important – that he did not intend to express universal truths in his poetry; secondly, that his images were used chiefly for sensuous immediacy, when often the reader is compelled to abstract the functional aspect of an image and leave the sensuous aspects alone in order to make sense of the passage in which it occurs (e.g. the famous compasses exist merely as two joined limbs capable of describing a circle; that they are cold,

T.M.P.—E

hard, usually yellow, etc., if taken into account, could effectively wreck the poem).

The case against this earlier twentieth-century school of thought on metaphysical poetry was presented powerfully and, in my opinion, incontrovertibly by Miss Rosemond Tuve's *Elizabethan and Metaphysical Imagery*, which appeared in 1947. Elizabethans – who had been less favoured by the previous critical school – and Metaphysicals were now linked in a common obedience to the precepts of contemporary logic, rhetoric and poetic. The aim of poetry was truth; an image was important not for its content but purely for its function in clarifying the notion or object to which it referred. 'Sensuous immediacy' and 'definition of emotion' were post-Symbolist aims which had been wrongly read back into an age with entirely different preoccupations. To the earlier period Reality was metaphysical, and the poetic method was to universalise; to the later, Reality lay in sensuous and emotional experience and the method was to particularise. The moderns had wrongly assimilated the Metaphysicals to themselves. With this I almost wholly agree. Perhaps, however, out of concern for her main theme, the contrast of Renaissance and modern poetic, Miss Tuve tends somewhat to underestimate the subordinate difference between Elizabethan and metaphysical poetry, and her explanation of that difference I cannot accept. She suggests that a metaphysical conceit is 'an image based simultaneously on a number of predicaments or common places in logic' and 'framed with especial subtlety' (p. 264). 'Puzzling differences of the effect between "Elizabethan" and "Metaphysical" conceits are often explicable as differences between extended pursuit of a simple logical parallel and extended pursuit of a likeness by basing it on several logical parallels' (p. 294). Both these statements are true but, I believe, inadequate. 'I also find difficulty,' says Miss Tuve, 'in another familiar differentia for the Metaphysical conceit : "the unexpected bringing together of ideas that seem to have nothing in common". . . Our reactions really depend on the aptness of *the logical link which relates* the ideas, *for the given image*, and on how cunning the author may be in making us see it' (p. 326). I am not sure precisely what this means, but it seems to imply that the remoteness of the terms is no true differentia for the conceit and that the aptness of the logic by which the terms are connected does supply a true differentia. If this were so, we should react similarly to a conceit and to a geometrical theorem. Further, Miss Tuve believes that 'the logical complexity and conceptually functional use of the metaphysical image' (p. 335) owe something to Ramistic influence. But Ramus, with his belief that all logical relations are intuitively perceived, more probably leads to Puritan thought, and, with his identification of dialectical and rhetorical argument, demanding the same rigid adherence to truth in each, leads rather to Augustan poetry than to metaphysical, which, I hope to show, requires the Aristotelian latitude in using untruths in the interest of truth.

It will be seen that I accept Miss Tuve's fundamental position – that the Metaphysicals as well as the Elizabethans consciously adhered to the principles of logic, rhetoric and poetic; and I do so with the deepest gratitude for what will surely prove to be one of the formative books in a revival of orthodox criticism. But I do not think she has given a satisfactory account of the nature of metaphysical wit and conceit, and in what follows I hope to supplement and somewhat to rectify her account of metaphysical poetry by means similar to her own, that is by going to contemporary theorists. Miss Tuve has no reference to the writers on wit, and it is to them that I turn for further light. At this point I must make clear that, although the account I shall give should help to differentiate between Elizabethans and Metaphysicals *in general*, it is quite wrong to regard metaphysical wit as only to be found among the so-called 'Metaphysicals'. With them it is a conscious and constant preoccupation, as it dominated every aspect of aristocratic society in the first half of the seventeenth century: sermons and essays, as well as the poetry of sacred and profane love; painting and sculpture, with their use of allegory; the extensive employment of emblems and *imprese*; the misinterpretation of Homer and hieroglyphs; the language, wittily obscure, of heavenly portents, of animals, birds and flowers; the baroque garden with its mechanical contrivances, its topiary, its statues and fountains with appropriate mottoes, its flowered sundials (living conceits, as Marvell shows); the triumphs, progresses, weddings, all masque-like, emblematic, *significant*. But there is wit, too, among the Elizabethans, though it is usually more obvious and traditional, and it can be traced back through Petrarch to the *dolce stil novo*, especially Cavalcanti and Cino de Pistoia, and behind them to the troubadours. Medieval Latin hymnody also used conceits, and both sacred and secular lines run further back to the other great age of wit under Imperial Rome, when conceited expression was at a premium among pagan orators and poets in Greek and Latin, and when the Fathers of the Church gave added depth to the mode by clothing with it the profound paradoxes of a faith founded upon God made man. The ultimate source of wit is God himself, as seventeenth-century theorists maintain; the proximate and local source would seem to be Alexandria, home of the scholiasts, of Philo, of S. Clement, Origen, and S. Athanasius. The present essay is merely an interim report, its conclusions tentative, but I believe it will sometime become clear that the whole European movement of 'baroque wit' or 'metaphysical conceit' originated in a Jesuit revival of patristic wit – first appearing in Spanish sermons of the sixteenth century, I imagine.

The seventeenth century produced in England a fine body of metaphysical writing but virtually nothing on the theory of wit, nor do I know of anything important in France, where the early dominance of neoclassicism reduced the metaphysical mode to a relatively superficial *préciosité*. Spain, where the mode flourished with least opposition, yields one important treatise on the subject, and Italy, always the home of critical debate, has several. I shall confine my attention to two works, one Spanish, one Italian. Baltasar Gracián's *Agudeza y Arte de Ingenio (Conceit and the Art of Wit)* appeared in 1642 and, revised and augmented, in 1648. Gracián, a Jesuit, is recognised by Spanish scholars as a distinguished writer. His various works on religious, moral and political themes have been translated into several languages, including English. Only the *Agudeza* defies translation. It consists of a series of 'discourses' on wit, illustrated with many complete poems and sizeable passages in verse and prose, drawn from a wide range of authors, Latin, Spanish, Portuguese and Italian, and forming a very valuable, but hardly translatable, anthology of witty writing.

Gracián's work is available in modern editions and is familiar enough to students of Spanish. It is not so easy to find a copy of Emanuele Tesauro's *Il Cannocchiale Aristotelico (The Aristotelian Perspective-Glass)*, first published in 1654, constantly reissued in the seventeenth century, but appearing no more after the early eighteenth. The work is dealt with by Croce, not, however, with great enthusiasm or understanding, in an essay, *I Trattatisti Italiani del Concettismo e Baltasar Gracián* (1899), and has brief mention in Professor Mario Praz's *Studies in Seventeenth-Century Imagery*, I (1939), which, being restricted to emblem literature, presents no occasion for a full treatment of Tesauro's theory. Gracián and Tesauro deserve the attention of students of English, as well as Continental, metaphysical poetry. Conceited writing was a craze spread throughout Europe, and, although poetry did not surrender its national characteristics even in the Baroque age, the element of wit in it is certainly international in its thought processes and in the common pool of

conceits from which all writers drew (Guarini wielded the compasses considerably before Donne). National differences appear
in the degree of seriousness or levity or fantastication with which
wit is employed, and in the various other poetic ingredients; but
Gracián and Tesauro are engaged with the general nature and
specific modes of the conceit rather than the wider functions of
literary criticism, so that what they have to say applies almost
as much to English as to Spanish or Italian poetry. There is, of
course, no suggestion that they are 'sources' of anything or
'influences' upon anybody. But, coming as they do after Europe
had been soaked for half a century in metaphysical wit, we might
expect them to articulate the methods by which poets and other
writers had been perhaps only half-consciously working. At least
they are more likely to assist our approach to seventeenth-
century wit than are those modern writers, however brilliant,
who rely on critical methods divorced from historical learning.

II

Menéndez Pelayo in his *Historia de las Ideas Estéticas en España*
(1947) says that Gracián wished 'to substitute for the purely
formal rhetoric of the schools, for the rhetoric of tropes and
figures, another *ideological* rhetoric, in which the conditions of
the style might reflect the qualities of the thought and give body
to the most involved conceptions of the mind'. Gracián takes a
very high view of conceit: it is 'the food of the soul', its production 'the occupation of cherubim and the elevation of men,
since it raises us to an extravagant hierarchy'. He attempts a description by analogy: 'what beauty is for the eyes and harmony
for the ears, that the conceit is for the understanding'. It is not
just a verbal trick but a statement about the objective nature of
things: 'All the intentional faculties of the soul, I mean those that

perceive objects, enjoy a certain artifice in them ['artifice': the result of art; in a good sense, as normally in the seventeenth century; referring here to the creative art in nature itself]; proportion among the parts of the visible is beauty; among sounds, harmony. . . . The understanding, then, as the first and chief faculty is delighted with the highest form of artifice, with the extreme of precision, in all the differences of objects.' The arts are concerned with these 'artifices', thought corresponding with things. 'Dialectic attends to the connection of terms, in order properly to form an argument, a syllogism, and rhetoric to the adornment of words, in order to compose a flower of eloquence, that is, a trope, a figure.' Wit is to be distinguished from dialectic and rhetoric : it reflects the highest aspect of nature, since it consists itself 'in artifice'. 'The wit is not content with truth alone, as the judgment is, but aspires after beauty. It would be a small thing in architecture to assure solid construction if one were to pay no attention to adornment.' Gracián equates 'adornment' with 'symmetry', surely meaning that beauty which he has already defined as consisting in 'proportion among the parts', and this is analogous with the artifice of the conceit, the beauty pursued by wit – the beauty, presumably, of *order*. The main definition follows : 'This conceited artifice, then [we remember that artifice is itself found *in* nature; it is 'discovered, not devised'], consists in a subtle concord, in a harmonic correlation among two or three extreme knowables, expressed by an act of the understanding.' And the conceit 'is an act of the understanding that expresses the correspondence which subsists among the objects'. 'Conceited artifice' is the artifice in nature as expressed by the understanding : 'conceit', the act of expressing it. 'Extreme knowables' agrees with the generally accepted account of the conceit, against Miss Tuve : it is the bringing together of things remote.

Gracián next distinguishes between 'wit of perspicacity', which seeks to discover difficult truths and is the ground of all the arts and sciences, and 'wit of artifice', which pursues 'subtle beauty', is more delightful as the other is more useful, and is not restricted to any specific discipline (which is what I think he means by saying that it has 'no fixed house'). He does not say, with some moderns, that wit of artifice – the sort we are dealing with – has nothing to do with truth; he does say that it is concerned with beauty and does not care 'so much about' difficult truths.

Another division follows, between 'conceptual wit, which consists more in the subtlety of the thought than in the words' and 'verbal wit, which consists more in the words, in such a way that if one departs from them the meaning disappears also, nor can they be translated into another language; of this type are equivoques. . . .' After these general remarks and broad distinctions, the rest of the treatise is devoted mainly to the classification of conceits, some founded on tropes, others not, each type illustrated by quotations which are carefully analysed. Croce could not perceive any principle of classification; and perhaps in this instance he was right. Gracián is a 'practical critic' rather than a theorist, though a critic of wit rather than literature. His account of the various types of conceit deserves close study but, being set out in no ascertainable order, is impossible to summarise. Discourse IV presents a characteristic heading : 'Of the first type of conceit, by correspondence and proportion', of which one illustration is a passage of Góngora :

> Extremo de las hermosas
> Y extremo de las crueles;
> Hija al fin de sus arenas
> Engendradoras de sierpes.

[Extreme among the beautiful and extreme among the cruel; daughter, to the last, of thy sands, begetters of serpents.]

A proportionate correspondence subsists between the beauty of the woman and of her native district, and between her cruelty and its cruelty in breeding vipers. The next heading is 'Of the conceit of improportion and dissonance' – and so forth. Discourse VI is especially interesting: 'Of the conceit by way of mysterious pondering' or 'pondering of a mystery'. An example is given from an unnamed 'modern writer on the excellences of the Empress of Heaven', who posed the question why Our Lady should be born and die at Nazareth and not in any other city of Palestine. 'It was, no doubt, because Nazareth means City of Flowers, for wherever this great Lady reigns is wholly changed into Paradise, the most frozen heart into spring, the thorns of faults into the flowers of virtues, and indeed everything blossoms where Mary is born.'

Gracián always insists that wit is something other than dialectic or rhetoric: 'Not any sort of simile (in the opinion of many) contains in itself subtlety and passes for a conceit, but only those which include some further form of mystery, contrariety, correspondence, improportion, sententiousness, etc.' 'Wit also has its arguments, but such that, if effectiveness rules in dialectic and eloquence in rhetoric, in these it is beauty.' Wit, then, is to be assessed finally, not on the validity of the argument involved, or even on the verbal graces with which it is adorned, but on the beauty which, as we have seen, being perceived by the understanding as it contemplates the ordered art of nature, has been expressed in the conceit....

III

Emanuele Tesauro professes to found his theory of wit on Aristotle. He not only adopts the Aristotelian categories but constantly refers to other works of 'the Philosopher', especially the *Rhetoric* and the *Poetics*. Nonetheless, working within a scheme of thought which is Christian, of the Counter-Reformation, and also probably influenced by Italian Neoplatonists of the sixteenth century, he contrives to produce a view of poetry very different from Aristotle's and consistent with a system of literary values by which the age of Marino can be hailed as the modern equivalent of the age of Augustus. His illustrations, chiefly from Classical and Silver Latin, are intrinsically much less interesting than Gracián's. He excels, rather, in the elaboration of his general and theoretical analysis, though at times commenting on verbal details with a subtlety and at a length that modern exponents of the latest line on dramatic imagery could scarcely emulate.

Like Gracián, Tesauro begins at the theological end. Wit is a 'vestige of the Deity in the human mind'; 'the angels themselves, Nature, the great God, in reasoning with men, have expressed with conceits, either verbal or symbolic, their most abstruse and important secrets.' The wit of God is found in the tropological, allegorical and anagogical significances of Holy Scripture and also in action, as in the Birth of Our Lord under *Augustus*, in the time of the *pax Romana*, etc. Not only God himself but also angels and demons have made direct use of conceits : the ambiguities of pagan oracles are demonic. 'This is traditional, but a good deal insisted on about this period; cf. the 'Nativity Ode'. It provides a gloss on the witches' ambiguities in *Macbeth*.) Also God makes conceits indirectly in Nature : this comprehends astrological significances, portents, the moralisation of animals and flowers – the usual elaborate pattern of meanings now grown familiar to students of the Elizabethans. The universe is, as it were, written over in the language of a wit which is, directly or indirectly, with or without perversion, derived from God : 'whatever the world has of wit either is God or is from God.' And man by his 'perspicacity' penetrates into the circumstances of every subject, distinguishing substance, matter, form, etc., and by his 'versatility' of mind 'swiftly confronts all these circumstances one with another or with the subject; ties them together or divides them; increases or diminishes them; deduces one from another; understands one through another; and with marvellous dexterity puts one in place of another. . . . And this is Metaphor, mother of poetry, of conceits, of ingenious notions, symbols and *imprese*'. Tesauro implies, I think, that man, with his own divinely-derived wit, not only appreciates the conceits already fully written in the book of nature but forms conceits of his own from what is present in nature only potentially, piecing together the scattered letters into meaningful phrases. Thus, as with Gracián, we have an objective theory of wit; it is 'discovered, not devised'; it is not a mere quirk of the human mind but has metaphysical and theological validity. Yet, in treating the conceited type of sermon, Tesauro distinguishes it from 'the rhetorical persuasion of scholasticism', which is speculative. However it may serve itself of scholastic materials and methods, this wit philosophy is not to be confused with the philosophy of the schools. Rather it was offered as a substitute for the elaborate and specialised scholastic system to the seventeenth-century gentleman, who aspired after learning yet had not so much time to devote to its acquisition as had the dedicated ecclesiastic. Though it may seem complicated to our own age, which flees from complication of all kinds except the mechanical, we must recognise that Tesauro's system, albeit orthodox and of the Counter-Reformation, shares this much with the independent philosophers and experimental scientists of the same period : it was intended to simplify its subject and render it more accessible – in this instance to the gentlemen of parts. It is, then, neither medieval nor modern but something between the two, partaking of both yet *sui generis* : a philosophy of the Baroque, of *secentismo*.

Like Gracián, Tesauro complains that there has been no systematic treatment of wit, and it is at pains to distinguish the study from mere rhetoric : 'Every conceit is a figured speech, but not every figured speech is a conceit.' His technical exposition of the nature of wit begins with a sentence already quoted : the mother or source of conceits is metaphor. Enlarging upon a well-known passage in the *Poetics* (1459a), he describes metaphor as 'the most witty and acute, the most strange and wonderful, the most cheerful and useful, the most eloquent and prolific offspring of the human intellect. Most witty, truly, because if wit consists (as we say) in binding together the remote and separate notions of the proposed objects, this is exactly the function of metaphor, and not of any other figure; since, drawing the mind, and not only the word, from one genus to another, it expresses one concept by means of another very different one; finding similarity in things dissimilar.' Tesauro agrees with Gracián (against Miss Tuve) in defining wit as a binding together of the remote. All metaphor does this more or less, but 'the metaphor is more witty and acute when the notions are very remote'. 'No one has saluted eloquence from afar who has not often heard that rhetorical figure PRATA RIDENT, meaning *prata vernant, amena sunt*. In truth this is not a real conceit but a simple metaphor, prolific mother, however, of innumerable conceits. It is, then, a beautiful flower of rhetoric, but a flower to-day overblown and, so to say, trampled through the schools, so that it begins to stink. Whence if in your academic discourse you were to prank yourself up with this metaphor as it were naked, PRATA RIDENT, you would see men laugh, not meadows. Similarly it makes us laugh to hear *the liquid crystals* and *the rays of Phoebus*.' He then demonstrates in how many ways the old metaphor can be revivified as wit : *Pratorum* HILARITAS *homines hilarat* is one of about a hundred variants that he invents, all offspring of the one mother metaphor.

This multiplication of conceits from a pre-existent metaphor is not haphazard but systematic, and the would-be wit is given precise instructions for mass-producing them. More important than the rules for such merely verbal operations, however, are Tesauro's elaborated methods of deriving metaphors from the contemplation of objects. Eight types of metaphor are distinguished.

(1) The metaphor of Proportion or similarity rapidly lets you know an object by means of its like. The more ingenious metaphors of this type work not univocally but by analogy, as between physical and moral, concrete and abstract, corporal and spiritual (e.g., Cicero calls the metaphysical substance of an oration, SANGUIS ET NERVI *orationis*).

(2) The metaphor of Attribution goes not from like to like but to something 'conjoined', as when the olive is called ARBOR *Palladis*, or the pearl *candidatus* LAPIS (the *matter* alone standing here for the subject). These are the most important types of metaphor – they appear, of course, in Aristotle's *Rhetoric* and *Poetics* (1411a and 1457b respectively) – and from them the other six can be derived as sub-species, 'accessories or 'tributaries', in the phrase of Tesauro. I shall run over them, giving one of Tesauro's examples of each. We have metaphor.

(3) Of Equivocation: *Si* APRUM *occideret* (Apro being a person as well as a boar);

(4) Of Hypotyposis – for vividness: Rebellion raises its *head*;

(5) Of Hyperbole: love being metaphorically fire, it may wittily become 'a portable furnace';

(6) Of Laconism: He died greater than he lived (i.e., because his neck was stretched);

(7) Of Opposition: *Sed fuit in* TENERA *tam* DURA *superbia forma* (The opposites clarify one another, and at least one of them is tropological);

(8) Of Deception: it was said of a prodigal that *Hic omnia*

sua distribuit pauperibus – MERETRICULIS (There must be a pause before the last word).

It will be observed that these sub-types are distinguished by the attributive use of rhetorical terms: thus a metaphor of hyperbole differs from a simple hyperbole in being tropical, as all wit, according to Tesauro, must be.

Each type of metaphor may be further sub-divided according to the categories of Aristotle. The following are all of proportion; the numbers show Tesauro's grouping of the ten categories into eight:

(1) Substance: tears as hot *rain* from the eyes;

(2) Quantity: a dwarf as an animated *atom*;

(3) Quality: the flowing *crystals* of the brooks;

(4) Relation: Pluto as *Infernum* IOVEM;

(5/6) Action and Passion: The mountains *grow white-headed; Genus omne humanum mortalitate* DAMNATUR (a judicial metaphor);

(7/9) Site and Place-and-Movement: *In Tiberis ripa* SEDET *Roma* (site); the tomb as *hard couch of the dead* (place); FLUUNT *per colla comae* (movement);

(8) Time: manhood ('la Virilità') described as AUTUMNITAS *hominis;*

(10) Habit (i.e., clothing): the green grass *impearled* with dew.

Of metaphor we must lastly note that 'the object signified by proper [i.e., non-metaphorical] terms imparts nothing but itself; but that signified through metaphor imparts two objects at one time, one within the other'. Man naturally desires to know much without great fatigue, says Tesauro, which is one, not very serious, way of explaining a preference for the 'concrete' style.

This matter requires elucidation. Let us take the metaphorical statement, 'Cleopatra is a serpent'. The ante-Tuvian critics would comment: 'This is better than an abstract characterisation because we have two objects presented instead of one [the arithmetical aspect], and because the snake-suggestions, slipperiness, elusiveness, even a hint of the repellent, vividly build up a realisation of Cleopatra's many-sided nature, while giving the prose a concrete, local life' [the importance of the sensory]. Miss Tuve would say that the only function of the serpent is to explain Cleopatra, and would probably add that the relevant serpent characteristics would be those of the bestiary rather than of sense-experience. She would undoubtedly point out that the image must be limited in application, e.g., that it does not imply Cleopatra's ability to enter a room by way of the crack under the door. Tesauro would agree with Miss Tuve except for one thing: he would maintain that Cleopatra also explains the serpent and that the reader is interested in both: it is the pattern of relations, 'two objects at one time, one within the other', which constitutes the nature and the beauty of the conceit. If the serpent merely explains Cleopatra it is a rhetorical serpent, but when a mutual serpent–Cleopatra relation is set up we have to do with wit. Metaphor, we remember, is the mother of conceits: in its essential pattern it is witty. But not all metaphor is witty, e.g., PRATA RIDENT. It would seem that when it has become conventional, it is rhetorical, capable of illustrating the subject but no longer expressing a mutual objective relationship. 'The raging sea' is, for example, a mere metaphor adequately descriptive but no longer suggesting a relationship between the sea and a mad-or-angry man-or-beast. 'Cleopatra is a serpent' would, however, be wit. A further and related point, that 'the metaphor of proportion is founded on the similarity of two subjects of different kinds by way of a certain *analogical propriety*', links Tesauro's theory of metaphor with his cosmological and theological view of wit, with, in fact, the 'Elizabethan world picture' and its now familiar correspondences.

It might be well at this point to clear up what looks like disagreement between Gracián and Tesauro. Gracián classifies some conceits as metaphorical, some not; Tesauro grounds all conceits in metaphor. The explanation is that Gracián uses 'metaphor' in its normal rhetorical sense, whereas Tesauro, investigating the precise nature of wit, finds an element of trope, of 'feigning' or fiction, in it all, even where there is no formal rhetorical figure of metaphor. Take Góngora's lady, who resembled her native, serpent-breeding sands. There is no formal metaphor : she is called beautiful and cruel, but she is not, like Cleopatra, called a serpent. (She *is* called daughter of the sands and this is a metaphor, if pedantically taken; but such forms – like 'a daughter of England' – are so common as scarcely to deserve the name, and Gracián does not recognise it as such). Now, Tesauro would say about this passage that, although there is no formal metaphor, the cruelty of a mistress (which, of course, is what is meant here) and the cruelty of a serpent are not univocally related but only *per analogiam*, i.e., by metaphor of proportion in the category of quality, and involving the equation of a moral and a physical attribute. Indeed, it would be more exact to say that 'cruel' is applied in different *tropical* senses to the woman and to the serpents, neither party being literally cruel, in the sense in which a thumb-twisting bully deserves the epithet.

All wit, then, according to Tesauro, is founded in metaphor, though not all metaphor is wit; novelty and the remoteness of the terms involved are the two criteria of wit so far established. But we have not yet attained the perfect conceit. For Tesauro distinguishes three ascending grades of conceit, corresponding to the three operations of the intellect. The first operation produces simple metaphor, which is what we have so far dealt with, and which may or may not be witty in accordance with the criteria already expressed. The second is allegory, 'that is, the continuation of simple metaphor'; e.g., 'One brief hour snatches from the queen of flowers her purple mantle and her crown.' This is the ordinary 'extended conceit'. But the third and highest operation of the intellect is that which produces argument, so that the perfect conceit must necessarily take an argumentative form. By induction from examples and inspired by what Aristotle says of enthymeme in the *Rhetoric* and elsewhere (1358a, etc.), Tesauro finally asserts that perfect conceits take the form of ARGUMENTS URBANELY FALLACIOUS. Some comments are necessary. First as to 'arguments', we have seen why this is the highest mode of conceit and we must remember from what has gone before that to be conceited at all an argument must be tropical. The specific mode of argument is by enthymeme: we are expected to know from Aristotle that this in rhetoric corresponds to the syllogism in dialectic; it is, in fact, a compressed syllogism founded on probable opinion rather than philosophical certainty. Next, as to 'fallacious', Tesauro states that not every ingenious argument is witty: a theorem of Euclid or a scientific explanation is ingenious without being witty. This is where Miss Tuve's explanation of the conceit fails, with its exclusive stress on the 'logical link'. By induction from examples Tesauro shows 'that the conceited argument has its power from wit, i.e. by way of a certain *cavilling fiction*'. He instances Martial's epigram on the bee in amber, *Credibile est ipsam sic voluisse mori*, an abbreviated enthymeme, which looks much less convincing in its full syllogistic form :

> All bees that have died in amber have wished so to die
> This bee has died in amber ;
> Therefore it has wished so to die.

Tesauro observes that it involves two fallacies. There is first a

paralogism *ex signo*, i.e., from the single instance : it would re-
quire a great many more bees stuck inside amber to render such
an argument, probable. Secondly, we have an argument *a falsa
analogia*, in the pretence that animals can think like men.
Here, it seems to me, is Tesauro's second great discovery. The
first was that wit is always tropical (founded in metaphor); the
second, and closely related, discovery is that, when it involves
argument (as it does at its 'highest'), wit is always *fallacious*.
Further light will be thrown on this question if we consider the
middle word of our definition, 'urbanely'. We have already seen
Tesauro distinguish wit from rhetoric. But in some respects it is
like rhetoric and unlike dialectic. And because of this the use
of fallacy may be justified. Urbane and dialectical cavillation are
contra-distinguished in the following respects : –

(1) in *Matter*. 'The matter of rhetoric comprehends civil
affairs in so far as they are morally persuasible', whereas 'the
matter of dialectic comprehends things scholastically disputable
among investigators of the truth'.

(2) in *End*. 'For, just as rhetoric has regard to popular persuasion and dialectic to scholastic instruction; so urbane cavillation has for its aim to delight the mind of the hearers with
playfulness without incumbrance of the truth [This means 'without getting in the way of the truth', not 'without burdening
oneself with the truth', as appears from what follows under (4)]
but dialectical cavillation has for its end to corrupt by a sort of
legerdemain the understanding of the disputants with falsity.'

(3) in *Material Form*. The urbane uses variety of style; the
dialectical uses a 'clear' style.

(4) in *Essential Form* : 'For if indeed every cavillation is a
fallacy, it is not therefore true that every fallacy will be an
urbane cavillation, but only that which, without false guile,
pleasantly imitates the truth but does not oppress it; imitates the

false in such wise that the truth appears by way of it as through a veil: so that from what is said you quickly understand what is not said; and in that rapid comprehension (as we have shown) is placed the true essence of metaphor. Hence, just as in simple metaphors, when I say to you *Prata rident* I do not intend to make you believe that the meadows snigger like men, but that they are pleasant, so the metaphorical enthymeme argues one thing so that by it you may understand another.'

From all this it emerges triumphantly that 'I conclude the URBANE ENTHYMEME to be *a witty cavillation in civil affairs; pleasantly persuasive; without the full form of the syllogism; founded upon a metaphor.* And this is that *most perfect conceit* of which we are discoursing in this place'.

The whole of this theory clearly depends on maintaining the Aristotelian distinction between rhetoric and dialectic as two different disciplines with different modes of argument and different degrees of rigour required in proof, and on the Aristotelian view that sophisms, although inadmissable in dialectic, are justifiable in rhetoric, where, however, they must be used to persuade only to honest courses. Ramus denied these distinctions and asseverated that the same strict rules of logical truth must be applied in rhetoric as in dialectic, so reducing the distinctive subject-matter of rhetoric to the use of figures (as in his disciple, Abraham Fraunce). Not that the looser, rhetorical argument was necessarily disallowed by Ramus; it was at times logically justified, rendered dialectical, as in the argument from special to general which, according to Miss Tuve, underlies much metaphysical wit: e.g., Donne's statement 'that the brittleness of the jet ring can *say* or *speak* a property of his lady's heart'. But if this is taken Ramistically, it is not wit but science; it remains wit only while its foundation is Aristotle and its process dialectically fallacious. The question is, did Donne really believe one

could learn about a girl's heart from a jet ring, or did he merely
pretend that this was so, in order to emphasise a piece of knowledge very differently acquired? If the latter, the process is not
Ramistic. Ramus, I think we can say, has much to do with neoclassicism, with the high value it places on poetic judgement and
its preference for a content derived from some non-poetic
study: cf. the innumerable didactic poems from Blackmore's
Creation to Grainger's *Sugar-Cane*. But he has nothing to do
with metaphysical wit. All wit is tropical; all wit in the form of
argument is deliberately fallacious, and so presented as to state
a truth by implication. I believe this to be a just analysis and that
the modern critic must avail himself of it in order to understand
metaphysical poetry aright.

Tesauro continues his relentless investigation in a series of
triads which are less original, of less practical moment and, to
the unaccustomed modern mind, probably more confusing than
helpful. There are three types of the perfect conceit, adductive,
deductive and reflective; they have three final causes, demon-
strative, deliberative and judicial; and three material causes,
the honest, the useful, the just; there are three manners of persuasion possible, the rational, the moral, the pathetic. Students of
rhetoric will recognise these triads; they complete the picture but
add no new insight. I should like now to gather together a few
important points scattered in various contexts up and down
Tesauro's lengthy treatise.

(1) Metaphor unites the three virtues of brevity (one word
contains more than one idea), novelty (it is a new word in relation to what it signifies) and clarity: 'the novelty causes wonder,
which is an intent reflection, impressing the conceit on your mind.'
The purpose of obscurity is clarity: 'For if a certain metaphor is
not perhaps easy for you to penetrate at first sight, as enigmas
and laconisms, nonetheless, when you have penetrated it, you see

that conceit much more clearly and have it more fixed in mind than if it had been spoken to you in ordinary words.' There is thus no love of obscurity for its own sake, nor is any obscurity intended to remain after an attentive reading. Obscurities are to be clarified by the intellect, not joyously embraced by the unconscious.

(2) Images can be used in two ways, as simile or as metaphor: simile compares, but metaphor feigns the identity of the objects. The former is appropriate to oratory, the latter to poetry, 'the essence of poetry being fiction'. 'Fiction' is Tesauro's rendering of Aristotle's *mimesis* and is legitimate, I think. Poetry gives 'instead of truth, verisimilitude'. But this verisimilitude is itself founded 'on the natural', and so must be related to truth; there is no contradiction between what is said here and what was previously said about truth expressed by fallacy. And Nature is stated to be 'more noble than art, since it is a work of the Divine Mind': the Renaissance theory of the continuity of art and nature is thus rejected, probably on account of the doctrine of the Fall, and preference given to a theory more akin to the Romantic – but we must not pursue the large question of cultural history adumbrated here.

(3) Concerning the matter of poetry, Tesauro justifies the use of the obscene, if a modest veil of figured and witty language is employed and if the aim is the free exercise of the writer's wit. The process itself is figured as 'gathering from the mud the jewels of a noble art' and a bold theological parallel follows: '. . . the human mind participates in the Divine, which with the self-same Divinity dwells in the marshes and in the stars, and from the most sordid made the most divine of corporeal creatures.' This should suggest a new approach to 'the immorality' of Donne, for example: not the flat-footed way of biography but a recognition of the constant baroque straining to bring the highest out of the lowest, itself a conceit with remotest terms, the

quasi-divine glory of wit discovered in the depths of iniquity.

(4) Tesauro distinguishes three types of audience: the ignorant, the erudite, and the popular, which is middling, a mixture of the other two. The last is the proper audience for *imprese*, which he regards as the most excellent embodiment of wit. Nonetheless, Tesauro obviously himself prefers what is addressed to a select audience (like Donne's 'understanders'), however he may object to the extremes of pedantry: 'But much more lively and erudite are those [conceits] that are taken with witty applications from the special and intrinsic theses of each science and art; whence they are agreeable to and understood by the erudite and not by the profane vulgar.' He lists jurisprudence, medicine, geometry, mathematics, music, arithmetic, grammar, painting, architecture, etc. – of all which frequent examples could be found among the English metaphysicals. Loyalty to Aristotle no doubt prevents him from discarding the traditional doctrine of the 'middle' audience, but the spirit of the age must have exerted a strong influence to bring in this praise of 'erudite' material; for the two attributes remain unreconciled, which is unusual in Tesauro's eminently tidy mind.

IV

Gracián and Tesauro can be happily conflated. Although their stresses are different, there are no real inconsistencies between them: it is merely that, especially in his understanding of the tropical nature of wit, Tesauro is the more profound theorist; Gracián being, however, more sensitive both to the individual instance and to the general aesthetic nature of wit. Here is a summary of their conflated teaching : –

(1) Conceits are founded in metaphor, always tropical, produced in three grades according to the three operations of the

intellect, and in the last grade invariably involve the statement of a truth by means of fallacy.

(2) Wit is distinct from Rhetoric: in Rhetoric the figure B exists solely to explicate the subject A, whereas in wit a mutual relationship AB is presented.

(3) Wit is also distinct from Dialectic: in aiming at persuasion; in its matter, drawn from civil affairs; in the legitimate use of fiction and fallacy; in the pursuit of beauty rather than difficult truths.

(4) The relation to truth must be clarified. The seventeenth century would not have understood those moderns who say that poetry has no concern with objective truth but only with the recording of personal experience or sensation. The purpose of Dialectic is to establish truth. Rhetoric is designed to persuade and may use fallacious dialectic to that end; but it must persuade only to that which is right – and which, therefore, could be demonstrated as right by true dialectic. Wit is not primarily concerned with truth but with beauty addressed to the understanding, yet it is only *more* concerned with beauty than truth; and, as the beauty aimed at is that of order as found in nature, this is, in any event, merely another aspect of truth. Wit expresses truth by way of fiction and fallacy.

(5) The relation to philosophy and theology is fundamental.

(a) Wit is exercised by God and is everywhere in nature, directly ('as the foreseeing God in creation had regard always to the redemption, so He made no natural work without its being a figure of some supernatural and evangelical mystery') and indirectly (to be assembled into conceits by the wit of man).

(b) The remote terms of a conceit are objectively related: the relationship is not imposed by the mind but discovered in nature, and is strictly metaphysical, since it arises expressly or implicitly from the wit of God.

(c) Human wit is thus a quasi-divine aptitude which apprehends relationships that are either expressed or exist potentially in nature through the wit of the Creator.

(d) As the object of wit is beauty, appealing to the intellect, i.e., that order, divinely constituted, which subsists among all the complex relationships of the universe, it would seem that the God-like wit of man produces an orderly yet surprising beauty in poetry, etc., as does God himself in creation. (Cf. the usual Elizabethan view of poetic and Divine creation as analogous.)

To what extent poets and other writers were conscious of this wit philosophy it is impossible to say. Gracián and Tesauro, coming after several decades of conceited practice, surely have the benefit of some previous thought; the system would hardly spring from their heads fully armed. And if the poets were conscious in their use of logic and rhetoric, it may well be that, in the more difficult and erudite matter of discovering relations between extreme terms in a universe theologically understood, they were employing some deliberate process derived from contemporary theory. The fact that in treating wit no distinction was made between prose and verse also hints at the possibility of a conscious process, for the prose-writer more than the poet tends to know what he is about. How much of the wit philosophy any particular writer was aware of is, however, a question that I see little hope of ever answering. It was, conscious or not, a daring and magnificent enterprise: to reveal the unity and order, and thus the beauty, of all God's creation – and an enterprise in which the least likely subject-matter might, with characteristic paradox, be expected to yield the most satisfying results. This is the dominant conceit of the age, the conceit about conceits: jewels in the mud, clearest proof of the omnipresent activity of God.

v

It would be unfair to conclude without some specimens of applied analysis.

(1) The greatest and most tremendous of all conceits is that in the *Vexilla Regis* of S. Venantius Fortunatus (though it may go back to some earlier patristic commentator):

> Arbor decora et fulgida,
> Ornata Regis purpurâ.

Our Lord's blood spread upon the Cross, to the eye of realism a pitiful and horrible spectacle, is by the eye of faith transformed into a regal splendour : 'adorned with the purple of the King.' Technically, this is of the first operation of the intellect, a metaphor of proportion in the category of habit; with the added complication that *purpurâ* is symbolic and *Regis* itself metaphorical, referring not to an earthly king but to God.

(2) Donne's compass conceit in 'A Valediction : Forbidding mourning' – it is best to see the old favourites in their new dress rather than to seek fresh examples – may represent the second operation of the intellect. It is a brief allegory, based on a metaphor of proportion (much the commonest type of metaphor in conceited use, I suspect), in the categories of action and place-and-movement.

(3) Of the third operation of the intellect there is an example in 'The Good-morrow' :

> What ever dyes, was not mixt equally;
> If our two loves be one, or, thou and I
> Love so alike, that none doe slacken, none can die.

This enthymeme is almost in full syllogistic form. Its major premiss is derived from a science rather than common opinion and thus appeals to the erudite; but it remains enthymematic, having only the status of probability. It presents a pretty collection of fallacies: (a) the fallacy *secundum quid*, since it shifts the ground from the physical field in which the major premiss is probably true, to the field of psychology in which there is no antecedent reason to believe that it applies; (b) *in dictione*, the fallacy of equivocation in the word 'one', since unity of loves is not a sense univocal with unity of substance; (c) the *secundum quid* could also be characterised as argument *a falsa analogia* between love and physical substances. But, although the analogy is not such as could form the basis of a valid argument in dialectic, yet there *is* a sort of analogy, a witty analogy by way of metaphor of proportion in the category of quality, which, with the fallacious enthymeme dependent upon it, indirectly yet vividly reveals a truth : the power of singleness in love.

Similarly in 'The Sunne rising' :

> Thine age askes ease, and since thy duties bee
> To warme the world, that's done in warming us.

The first phrase is a very compressed enthymeme, with precisely the same fallacies as above : *secundum quid* (shifting the ground from human old age to the age of the sun) or false analogy, with equivocation in the word 'age'. It is natural that these should be the commonest fallacies in metaphysical poetry : the attempt to link remote terms, to connect very different fields of discourse, gives rise to the interplay of two meanings in one verbal form, which is equivocation, and to the shifting of the proposition from one area of reference, where it is valid, to another, where it is logically invalid – the *secundum quid*. The rest of the quotation above also depends on the fallacy of equivocation, since the real world and lovers' 'world' are not univocally the same, but are related by metaphor of proportion in the category of substance. (The personification of the sun, giving rise to 'thine age askes ease', is, of course, metaphor of hypotyposis in the category of time.)

Lastly, we can now understand why, as Sir Herbert Grierson says, 'The Flea' 'was greatly admired as a masterpiece of wit' both in England and Holland. For here out of the lowest material springs the highest wit. The flea and the blood are physically objectionable (the point is *not* that Jacobeans didn't mind them!); the rhetorical purpose of the piece is a persuasive to fornication and is therefore morally objectionable. We shall examine only the chief aspects of the poem :

> Oh stay, three lives in one flea spare,
> Where wee almost, yea more than maryed are.
> This flea is you and I, and this
> Our mariage bed, and mariage temple is;

> . . . .

> Though use make you apt to kill mee,
> Let not to that, selfe murder added bee,
> And sacrilege, three sinnes in killing three.

The arguments involved in the above are in the usual form of the enthymeme urbanely fallacious, but they are especially dazzling because of the back and forth play between ordinary and tropical significances. The poem is powerful because it has the broad background of ancient (Old Testament) teaching about blood (Gen. 9 : 4), together with the mystery of sexual union and the supernatural mystery of the sacrament of marriage. 'This flea is you and I' because the blood is the life – an implied metaphor of attribution in the category of substance, but, as enthymeme, involving a double use of the fallacy of part for whole (blooddrops for persons; stomach-content for flea). It is 'our marriage bed', since copulation is 'mingling bloods': the truncated enthymeme has the familiar fallacy *in dictione*, equivocation; for 'bloods' is used tropically in speaking of copulation but literally in reference to the flea. It is also 'our marriage temple', since in church the twain become one flesh : the same fallacy is repeated. Next, the three crimes are argued enthymematically with the same fallacy in reverse, a false proceeding from tropical to literal : the flea is I, therefore to kill it would be murder; it is you, hence it would be suicide; it is a temple, hence its destruction would be sacrilege. The conclusion of the last stanza :

> Then learne how false, feares bee;
> Just so much honor, when thou yeeld'st to mee,
> Will wast, as this flea's death tooke life from thee—

is an enthymeme with the fallacy of *secundum quid*, since there is a manifest shifting of ground from the physical to the moral universe of discourse. What truth does the poem reveal? It vividly presents a true doctrine of marriage, in a surprising and therefore memorable form. But this is not its chief purpose; it is not primarily didactic in so limited a sense. And, of course, the ostensible, rhetorical purpose, the persuasive to fornication, is a conventional fiction and not its real purpose at all. What Donne achieves in 'The Flea', by the exercise of that greatest power of the human intellect, the quasi-divine spark of wit – and what constitutes the poem's true purpose or final cause – is a triumphant display of the subtle beauty with which certain remote terms, the equation of blood and life, lovers, a flea, a temple, are related, objectively and significantly, though not logically; for the flea is a valid symbol though not a proper basis for logical argument. In this way the poem instructs and delights with the presentation of an exquisitely ordered universe and the more because a beautiful order has been revealed in and through the least promising material : jewels among the mud.

SOURCE: *Northern   Miscellany   of   Literary   Criticism,* I (1953).

Joseph H. Summers

GEORGE HERBERT: THE CONCEPTION OF FORM (1954)

There is a certain irony in the fact that the most formal of seven-teenth -century Anglican poems have been so much enjoyed by the anti-formalists in religion and art. The appeal of George Her-bert's poetry to the opponents of ritual was a justifying triumph for Herbert's conception of form: in poetry as well as religion Herbert tried to work out a middle way between 'slovenliness' and 'superstition'. It was by means of form that the material could be used in the service of the spiritual, that the senses could be properly employed for the glorification of God.

The problem of the relationship between objects of the senses and Christian worship had been introduced with the beginning of the ritual in the ancient church. In Herbert's England the Puritans and the Catholics marked the limits of theory and practice.[1] For the extreme Puritan, the ritual and 'adornments' in the church were only sensuous barriers (similar to the priest's office) between the naked individual soul and God: the serious business of salvation left no room for them. It was, more-over, presumptuous for sinful man to attempt to honour God through the creation of formal beauty within God's house; the proper method of honouring God, the essence of worship, was to confess one's unworthiness, to pray for forgiveness and God's grace, and to preach the gospel. Christian poetry had its prac-titioners and its appreciative audience outside the services, and certainly most Puritan preachers believed that the art of logic and rhetoric (so long as they were not separated) were useful hand-maidens for the instruction and moving of their audiences. But the idea that ritual or 'ornaments' within the church could either aid the individual worshipper or honour God was alien to the largest segment of Puritan thought. The light of the Spirit should reach the individual directly, like sunlight through pure glass; it should not be contaminated by 'externals', as sunlight was coloured by the pictured windows of the Papists.

Certain Catholics embraced an opposite attitude which might seem equally 'enthusiastic' to a person who followed Hooker's tradition. In his *Spiritual Exercises* St Ignatius Loyola had stated that 'every meditation or contemplation about a bodily thing or a person, as for example, about Christ, demands the formation of a bodily place in vision',[2] and his widely practised 'application of the senses' was influential in increasing exactly those sensuous details of Catholic worship to which the Protestants objected. The rich liturgy, rather than obscuring the way to God, came to provide the chief light. The Protestants insisted that the Catholics' engrossment in the sensuous details of worship was divorced from reason, from an understanding of the symbolism : it was idolatry.

Many members of the Church of England tried to find a way between the extremes. George Herbert took a firm and consistent position. As a believer in the Covenant of Grace, he could never allow the ritual to become a substitute for incorporeal experience. Yet Herbert also believed that the individual should not present himself, publicly at least, in disorder before God. God should be worshipped in 'the beauty of holiness', and He had shown in the 'two Books of His Revelation' that the arrangement of 'objects of the senses' (whether things or words) into a pattern symbolic of divine order was the method of worship which pleased Him. It was also one of the most persuasive means by which men could be led to worship.

The ordering process was important in itself, and the Christian could create 'significant form' in the church even where traditionally none had been intended. Izaak Walton tells that in Herbert's reconstruction of the church at Leighton Bromswold, 'by his order, the Reading Pew, and Pulpit, were a little distant from each other, and both of an equal height; for he would often say, "They should neither have a precedency or priority of the other : but that *Prayer* and *Preaching* being equally useful, might agree like Brethren, and have an equal honour and estimation".'[3] Reason and taste substantiated formal construction at every step. Nicholas Ferrar agreed with Herbert about the proper design for a church, and Herbert undoubtedly agreed with Ferrar's opinion of extemporaneous prayers : *'As for extemporary prayers, he used to say, there needed little other confutation of them, than to take them in short-hand, & shew them sometime after to those very men, that had been so audacious to vent them. Ask, saith he, their own judgements of them (for I think they will hardly know them again), & see if they do not blame them'*[4]

The use of reason as confutation of the extemporaneous implied that the ritual itself must be rational. The individual who participated in the services must understand the signficance of each detail. According to Walton, Herbert's sermons at Bemerton were often devoted to a meticulous explanation of Anglican formal practice. The individual should understand the rational 'fitness' of every phrase of the service, and he should apply that understanding to his own life. He should even know why particular passages of Scripture were read on particular days. He must understand the 'reasons' for all the Holy Days and the symbolic significance of every physical movement of the priest and the congregation.

Walton described the times when Herbert was 'too zealous' : 'And to this I must add, That if he were at any time too zealous in his Sermons, it was in reproving the indecencies of the peoples behaviour, in the time of Divine Service; and of those Ministers that hudled up the Church-prayers, without a visible reverence and affection; namely, *such as seem'd to say the Lords prayer, or a Collect in a Breath*; but for himself, his custom was, to stop betwixt every Collect, and give the people time to consider what they had pray'd, and to force their desires affectionately to God, before he engag'd them into new Petitions.'[5] In the years at Bemerton Herbert appropriately reserved his outbursts of 'passion and choler' for those who obscured the meaning of form. Such men offended both God and God's little ones. For the ritual could become a means of Grace. If every aspect of it was understood, it could teach the way of salvation and the beautiful pattern of God's creation. Proper worship resulted in an ethical and spiritual ordering of the worshipper's life. That was the ultimate method of honouring God.

Herbert's ideas were by no means original; it is difficult to ascribe to any one man – or civilization – the origins of the analogical habit of mind and the belief that order, measure, proportion and harmony are both divine and beautiful. He could have found most of the concepts in St Augustine, the only early Church father whose works he mentioned in his will. Karl Svoboda has insisted that Augustine's 'aesthetic system' is the 'most complete' that antiquity has handed down to us : it is 'the crowning synthesis of the ancient aesthetic'.[6] But the most important factor for the Christians who followed was that Augustine's 'synthesis' was built around the central conception of the Christian God. Rightly understood, both ethics and aesthetics were only reflections (and not necessarily differing reflections) of the divine, creating Beauty :

What innumerable toys, made by divers arts and manufactures in our apparel, shoes, utensils and all sorts of works, in pictures also in divers images, and these far exceeding all necessary and moderate use and all pious meaning, have men added to tempt their own eyes withal; outwardly following what themselves make, inwardly forsaking Him by whom themselves were made, and destroying that which themselves have been made! But I, my God and my Glory, do hence also sing a hymn to Thee, and do consecrate praise to Him who consecrateth me, because beautiful patterns which through men's souls are conveyed into their cunning hands, come from that Beauty, which is above our souls, which my soul day and night sigheth after.[7]

The ideas of God as the Great Artificer and as Absolute Beauty were theological conceptions with inevitable aesthetic corollaries, and the work of art could be valued exactly because it reflected the divine pattern. The ethical life was beautiful, and an unethical life or poem by definition represented that lack of order called 'ugly' or 'evil' – not a positive quality, but an absence of the good and the beautiful. In so far as an object lacked those qualities or had them imperfectly, it lacked existence; for everything that truly existed, in the sense that it fulfilled its proper nature, was good.[8] Any object or fact could therefore become a first term for almost any number of 'true' metaphorical comparisons, since every 'existing' thing derived from and reflected the divine creation. Long before Donne's playful poem, Augustine contemplated the flea seriously as an 'aesthetic object'.

There was, of course, an ambiguity in Augustine's thought (as in that of the Greeks before him and the Christians after) concerning both the value and the role of beautiful objects of the senses. They could be mortally dangerous. In the same paragraph of *The Confessions* in which he had stated the divine origin of those 'beautiful patterns which through men's souls are conveyed into their cunning hands', Augustine had added, 'And I, though I speak and see this, entangle my steps with these outward beauties; but Thou pluckest me out, O Lord, Thou

pluckest me out; *because Thy loving-kindness is before my eyes.*
For I am taken miserably, and Thou pluckest me out mercifully;
sometimes not perceiving it, when I had but lightly lighted upon
them; otherwhiles with pain, because I had stuck fast in them'.
Man fulfilled his proper nature only through the glorification of
God. The fact that material objects of beauty had such power
to intoxicate the senses could lead even a man who recognized
the divine pattern in them to feel the danger of a sensuous engrossment without meaning and without God. It could also lead
him to attempt to suppress sensuous response. A number of men
in seventeenth-century England were not convinced, as
Augustine was, that it was an error 'to wish the whole melody of
sweet music which is used to David's Psalter, banished from my
ears, and the Church's too';[9] and there were Puritans who took
more seriously than Robert Burton the attitude implied by his formulation, 'And what is poetry itself, but, as Austin holds, the
wine of error administered by drunken teachers?'[10] God was a
spirit even though the Son had been incarnate, and one tradition
of Christianity indicated that the mature soul anticipated the
joys of heaven by rising above response to the matter of earth.

The more common emphasis, echoed throughout the seventeenth century, was that God's creation was second only to His
Word as a source of truth and enlightenment. The danger that
the individual might be blind to the truth of the created world,
that he might 'rest in Nature, not the God of Nature',[11] was real,
but it could be met. God had provided 'repining restlessnesse'
for the man who did not find Him :

> Not that he may not here
> Taste of the cheer,
> But as birds drink, and straight lift up their head,
> So he must sip and think
> Of better drink
> He may attain to, after he is dead.   ('Mans medley')

God could, moreover, grant the grace for man to perceive the essential relationships :

> Indeed mans whole estate
> Amounts (and richly) to serve thee :
> He did not heav'n and earth create,
> Yet studies them, not him by whom they be.

> Teach me thy love to know;
> That this new light, which now I see,
> May both the work and workman show :
> Then by a sunne-beam I will climbe to thee.

('Mattens')

One of poetry's greatest potential values was that God could employ it as a means through which man might perceive those relationships.

If poetry was an imitation of God's creation and possessed the divine power of moving the affections, the use of it for secular ends might come near to blasphemy. Although many Christians enjoyed secular or pagan poetry in a moral manner, there was little doubt that poetry with a Christian subject could be infinitely more pleasant and profitable. Not many men of the seventeenth century were buffeted black and blue by angels of God for their too great love of some profane writer as was St Jerome, but a precisian or parson with a vivid sense of his Christian calling might either abandon the arts of rhetoric and poetry entirely or consecrate their practice to the service of God.

To learn how poetry could be consecrated, Herbert had neither to engage in historical research nor to follow painfully those medieval writings which were read in his day. The religion, the poetry, and 'the arts' of his own day were filled with manifestations of the hieroglyphic view of the universe and of experience, a view which could be basic to the practice of the Christian poet and which contained within itself a formal principle. More important for Herbert than the general notion of the microcosm–macrocosm or even the continual example of the ritual was the Bible.

The ancient four-fold interpretation of the Scriptures, which had inspired so much of medieval allegory and symbolism and had served Dante well, was attacked during the seventeenth century as a barrier to the clear perception of those 'few things needful' to salvation and Christian charity. After all, some schoolmen had acknowledged seven and eight meanings, and such ingenuity obscured the simple 'real' meaning of God's Word. But the older habit of mind was too deeply ingrained to be easily erased. As hermeneutics became a weapon in ecclesiastical controversies, the men who attacked the earlier 'superstitious' interpretations sometimes derived the most metaphorical truths from their 'plain' reading of the Bible. Such an outcome was almost inevitable, for the Bible was filled with metaphors and parables and types, and it declared the cosmological significance of almost everything from the heavens to the ant. In 'Discipline' Herbert echoed the Protestant insistence that the Bible contained all knowledge and was a complete guide for every action in man's life :

> Not a word or look
> I affect to own,
>   But by book,
> And thy book alone.

The devout Christian attempted to 'apply' almost every passage in the Old and New Testaments to his own moral and spiritual condition :

> Oh that I knew how all thy lights combine,
>   And the configurations of their glorie !
>   Seeing not onely how each verse doth shine,
> But all the constellations of the storie.

This verse marks that, and both do make a motion
Unto a third, that ten leaves off doth lie :
Then as dispersed herbs do watch a potion,
These three make up some Christians destinie :
Such are thy secrets, which my life makes good,
And comments on thee : for in ev'ry thing
Thy words do finde me out, & parallels bring,
And in another make me understood.
Starres are poore bookes, & oftentimes do misse :
This book of starres lights to eternall blisse.

('The H. Scripture [II]')

Such an attitude made inevitable a symbolic exegesis of the text. The pattern for exegesis could be found in the Gospels, the Epistles of Paul, and the book of Hebrews, where it was shown how persons and events in the Old Testament had divinely prefigured the life of Christ and Christian doctrine and practice. There are references to almost every one of the specifically biblical types in Herbert's poetry. But once the method had been shown, neither the early Fathers nor the men of the seventeenth century were satisfied with the few types mentioned in the New Testament. Many discoveries of types were individual and eccentric; but there was general agreement, for example, that the twelve tribes of Israel had mystically prophesied the twelve Disciples, that Aaron's chief importance lay not in his historical role but in his embodiment of the type of God's priest, that the bride of The Song of Solomon was a type of the Church, the Bride of Christ. It is important to realize that the types were considered purposeful anticipations by God of the future unfolding of His Will, not merely imaginative analogies drawn by the reader :

For as the Jews of old by Gods command
Travell'd, and saw no town;
So now each Christian hath his journeys spann'd :

Their storie pennes and sets us down.
A single deed is small renown.
Gods works are wide, and let in future times;
His ancient justice overflows our crimes.

('The Bunch of Grapes')

The idea of the types could be extended to profane literature and could partially sanctify it. The structure of the universe and the nature of God's plan were so evident that even pagans had occasionally understood, however gropingly, many religious truths. Sure of the truth (like the Freudians of a later day), the Christian readers welcomed the perceptions of it which they found in classic mythology. Just as Paul had been able to tell the Athenians the identity of their Unknown God, so any educated reader could join Giles Fletcher in telling them the true identity of Orpheus or Zeus or Hercules:

Who doth not see drown'd in Deucalions name,
(When earth his men, and sea had lost his shore)
Old Noah; and in Nisus Lock, the fame
Of Sampson yet alive; and long before
In Phaethons, mine owne fall I deplore :
     But he that conquer'd hell, to fetch againe
     His virgin widowe, by a serpent slaine,
Another Orpheus was then dreaming poets feigne.

('Christs Triumph over Death', st. 7)

The general assumption that 'sensible images' 'shadowed' intellectual or divine conceptions, in the present as well as in the past, made for extraordinary formal parallels between religious and secular 'images', between, for example, the sacraments and the emblem books. Richard Hooker noted 'that many times there are three things said to make up the substance of a sacrament, namely, the grace which is thereby offered, the element which shadoweth or signifieth grace, and the word which expresseth what is done by the element',[12] and Rosemary Freeman has recently defined the tripartite formal structure of the emblem.[13] As a good Anglican of his time Herbert believed that 'The H. Communion' and 'H. Baptisme' were the only two sacraments which Christ had ordained for His Church; but that ordination had put the stamp of divine approval on that hieroglyphic practice which the Egyptians were believed to have known and taught to the Greeks, a practice which the emblem books, those best-sellers of their day, typified. Although most men of the seventeenth century would have been shocked by the comparison, the Protestants at least considered both the picture of the emblem and the element of the sacrament 'visible signs and symbols of internal and invisible things'. The elements or signs of the sacrament of communion were the bread and wine; the sign of the emblem was a literal picture, a representation of some symbolic figure or situation which could not be understood without the 'word' and the explanation. The 'word' of consecration of the communion service 'which expresseth what is done by the element' was paralleled by the 'mot' of the emblem, which summarized the bit of moral wisdom which the emblem was to inculcate. That wisdom as it acted on the reader, like the actual grace of the sacrament, had no precise material counterpart. But the emblem's poem, which explained the exact relationship between the motto and the picture and rationally applied the moral to daily life, paralleled the sermon of explanation which usually preceded the celebration of the communion. The emblem book in England, like the Protestant theory of the two sacraments, insisted that the symbol be rationally explained and 'applied'.

The insistence on the interrelations of spiritual reality, the symbol, the word, and the explanation was not confined to the sacraments and the emblem books. The painters, the musicians, and the poets expressed those relationships, sometimes lightly and sometimes seriously, even when by modern canons those expressions seemed to involve violations of the rules of their crafts.

Each developed varieties of what may be called hieroglyphic
form. Yet the composer no more attempted to convey the exact
'curve of the feeling' of God's 'exalting the humble and meek',
the experience of falling, or the voice crying out of the deep,[14]
than the poet tried to 'recreate the experience' of 'Trinitie Sun-
day', 'Easter-wings', or 'The Altar'. Various artists and
artisans did believe that symbolic representations which involved
more than one sense in apprehension increased the pleasure and
therefore the effectiveness of their works. That pleasure derived
less from a delight in man's artfulness than from a recognition of
the hieroglyphic nature of the universe.

Herbert had taken seriously the Lawyer's summary of the Law
and the Prophets : 'Thou shalt loue the Lord thy God with all
thy heart, and with all thy soule, and with all thy strength, and
with all thy minde, and thy neighbour as thy selfe' (Luke 10 :
27). His conclusion he phrased in the terms of St Paul : 'Let all
things be done decently, and in order', and 'Let all things be
done vnto edifying' (1 Cor. 14 : 40, 26). In *A Priest to the Temple*
that formulation applied specifically to the services of the
Church of England. The ritual of the Book of Common Prayer
was to be followed because it provided a decent, orderly and
edifying form of worship which reflected that ordered beauty of
the universe to which the individual strove to conform. In daily
life the same criteria applied. The command of love to God and
one's neighbour meant that each action must be decent, orderly
and edifying as well as charitable. It was impossible to distinguish the aims of specific actions, for all was done to the glory
of God : the aid both spiritual and physical of one's neighbour
was also an act of worship of the productive life; and any
individual act of public or private worship, once communicated,
could become an act of edification to one's neighbour. The
ultimate method of reflecting God's glory was the creation of a

work of decency and order, a work of beauty, whether a church, an ordered poem or an ordered life. This was not confined to the artist, but was the privilege and duty of every Christian. To do all actions 'as for thee' was 'The Elixir' 'That turneth all to gold'.

Herbert intended the poems in *The Temple* as expressions of his love for God as well as his neighbour. In Herbert's characteristic imagery, they are both 'fruits and flowers' of the Christian life, 'wreaths' of worship for God's altar and the harvest of 'fruits' of edification for others. As acts of worship they were to symbolize in their elaborate forms the beauty of the divine creation. As acts of edification they were to communicate to others the rational fitness of the symbolic forms, and to inflame them with the desire to follow the 'beauty of holiness'. The poems thus fulfilled for their readers the traditional classical aims, pleasure and profit. For nothing could be more pleasant than to contemplate the order of God's providence in the universe, the Church, or the personal life; and nothing could be more profitable, since such contemplation should increase the reader's faith and cause him to order his own life after the divine pattern.

Any attempt therefore to find either in individual poems or in the sequence of the poems a direct revelation of autobiography will fail, for the primary purpose of the poems was not what we understand by self-expression. There is, of course, no question of sincerity. The poems are a 'picture' of meticulously observed spiritual experience. But the self to Herbert was not the valuable thing which it became to a later age, and he desired that his poems should be burned if Ferrar did not think they could 'turn to the advantage of any dejected poor Soul'.[15] 'Personality' and personal experiences were of interest to the poet exactly in so far as they could be profitably used in the objective creations which were his poems. In his 'Dedication' to *The Temple* Herbert made a sharp distinction between his poems and himself, which still warns the reader:

>   Lord, my first fruits present themselves to thee;
>   Yet not mine neither : for from thee they came,
> And must return. Accept of them and me,
> And make us strive, who shall sing best thy name.
>   Turn their eyes hither, who shall make a gain :
>   Theirs, who shall hurt themselves or me, refrain.

For the conception which gives significance to the individual poems and to the organization of *The Temple*, a passage from one of Lancelot Andrewes's sermons is more revealing than most of the misty bits of Herbert's biography :

So come we to have two sorts of Temples; Temples of flesh and bone, as well as Temples of lime and stone. For if our bodies be termed houses, because our souls, tenant-wise, abide and dwell in them; if because our souls dwell they be houses, if God do so they be temples : why not? why not? . . . But then they be so specially when actually we employ them in the service of God. For being in His Temple, and there serving Him, then if ever they be *Templa in Templo*, 'living Temples in a Temple without life'. A body then may be a Temple, even this of ours.

And if ours, these of ours I say, in which the Spirit of God dwelleth only by some gift or grace, with how much better right, better infinitely, His body, Christ's, in Whom the whole Godhead in all the fulness of it, dwelt corporally ![16]

We do not need to assume that Herbert knew this particular passage, for the conception of the Temple was present everywhere in Christian thought. But the passage gives to the modern reader the key to the meaning of Herbert's title. For the temple as a building was a hieroglyph for the body, particularly the human body in the service of God and the divine body of Christ. By implication of its constructive elements, 'flesh and bone' and 'lime and stone', the temple could become a symbol for all the types of order in the universe, both God's and man's. It is that symbol which pervades Herbert's volume.

Herbert's inclusion of many poems which refer to actual cere-
monies or physical details of the English Church has led even so
perceptive a critic as Helen C. White, who recognized the
ambiguity of the title, to conclude that Herbert abandoned his
initial plan for the organization of his poems.[17] No one would
suggest that Herbert conceived of an abstract plan for something
resembling 'The Christian Year'. Yet the order of the poems in
the Williams MS. and the careful rearrangement of them in the
Bodleian MS. and the 1633 edition indicate that Herbert did
arrange the poems in what was to him a significant order which
had little to do with biographical revelation.[18] If we conceive of
The Temple as the symbolic record, written by a poet, of a
'typical' Christian life within the Church, most of Miss White's
perplexities concerning the meaning of the order of the poems
disappear. 'H. Baptisme', for example,[19] is a natural meditation
after 'Easter' and 'Easter-wings' for the Protestant who remem-
bers the symbolism of the death, burial and Resurrection; and
'Nature' and 'Sinne' almost inevitably follow with the reminder
that baptism does not free man from his sinful nature. 'Affliction (i)' is more personal than most of Herbert's poems, but it
also naturally follows 'Sinne'. 'Repentance', 'Faith', 'Prayer' and
'The H. Communion' are the means by which the Christian
triumphs over affliction, and they are followed by the general re-
joicing of 'Antiphon (i)' and the more specific expressions of
'Love (i)' and '(ii)'. The two poems called 'The Temper' are
prayers that God will not 'rack me . . . to such a vast extent',
following the exaltation of 'Love', and indicating the inevitable
emptiness after the moment of illumination. 'Jordan (i)' is Herbert's personal declaration of intent in writing his poems; the
poem relates directly to the prayer of 'Love (ii)', and its
general signficance is partially indicated by 'Employment (i)',
which immediately follows. The Christian unsure of his calling
turns to 'The H. Scriptures', is moved by the account of the

descent of the Holy Spirit on 'Whitsunday', and prays that similar 'Grace' may 'Drop from above'. Not all the sequences are so easily followed, but the central plan is clear. Long before Andrewes, Paul had indicated in 1 Cor. 6 : 19–20 that 'temple' had one primary meaning for the Christian. The Church of England, in its doctrines, its services and even the physical construction of its churches, furnished spiritual sustenance for that 'temple not made with hands', and it was filled with hieroglyphs of man's spiritual state. But it was the life of man within that Church which formed the principle of organization for Herbert's volume.

However symmetrical the ideal state of the Christian at any one moment, the pilgrimage of the Christian in time was not a broad and straight highway from the vales of sin to the Heavenly City. The very fluctuations between sorrow and joy, doubt and assurance, which caused George Herbert Palmer to believe that the arrangement of the poems was meaningless, seemed to the earlier readers of *The Temple* one of the most valuable evidences of Herbert's psychological realism. Most of the men of the seventeenth century did not believe that sorrow was totally banished or that man achieved continuous beatitude on this earth. God had constantly to 'create' :

> Lord, mend or rather make us : one creation
> Will not suffice our turn :
> Except thou make us dayly, we shall spurn
> Our own salvation.   ('Giddinesse')

Through Herbert's pictures of violently alternating spiritual change, however, they could perceive a deepening understanding of the 'giddie' state of man. It is significant that all of Herbert's 'Afflictions' (there are five poems so entitled, although only the first is generally known today) occur within the early part of 'The Church', the central body of lyrics within *The Temple*. Those 'Afflictions' represent a developing spiritual maturity in the attitudes which they express. In the larger half of 'The Church' the experience earlier described as 'Affliction' is comprehended under new modes : as the 'Dulnesse', 'Complaining', 'Longing', 'The Search' or 'Grief' of the individual; or as 'Discipline', 'The Pulley', 'The Crosse', part of 'Josephs coat', the 'Bitter-sweet' of the Christian life :

> Ah my deare angrie Lord,
> Since thou dost love, yet strike;
> Cast down, yet help afford;
> Sure I will do the like.
> I will complain, yet praise;
> I will bewail, approve :
> And all my sowre-sweet dayes
> I will lament, and love.

It was, perhaps, a perception of the pattern of *The Temple* which led T. S. Eliot to remark that Herbert's poetry 'is definitely an *œuvre* to be studied entire'.[20]

The form of Herbert's volume is often the key to the understanding of individual poems 'Love (III)', one of Herbert's best-known poems in the anthologies, has been generally interpreted as picturing the soul's welcome to the Communion or to salvation on earth :

> Love bade me welcome : yet my soul drew back,
> 　　Guiltie of dust and sinne.
> But quick-ey'd Love, observing me grow slack
> 　　From my first entrance in,
> Drew nearer to me, sweetly questioning,
> 　　If I lack'd any thing.
>
> A guest, I answer'd, worthy to be here :
> 　　Love said, You shall be he.
> I the unkinde, ungratefull? Ah my deare,
> 　　I cannot look on thee.
> Love took my hand, and smiling did reply,
> 　　Who made the eyes but I?

> Truth Lord, but I have marr'd them : let my shame
> Go where it doth deserve.
> And know you not, sayes Love, who bore the blame?
> My deare, then I will serve.
> You must sit down, sayes Love, and taste my meat :
> So I did sit and eat.

As the poem is in the Williams MS. it is probably 'early', but both there and in the 1633 edition it is the last lyric within 'The Church' and it follows 'Death', 'Dooms-day', 'Judgement', and 'Heaven'. George Ryley, who had read *The Temple* as the typical record of the Christian life, recognized that 'the matter of it is equally applicable to the entertainment we meet with in Divine ordinances'; but because of the position of the poem in *The Temple* he believed, correctly I think, that it was intended as a description of the soul's reception into heaven : 'A Christian's coming to Heaven is the effect of Divine Love. Therefore, after a contemplation on the state, it's proper to ruminate a little upon that which enstates us there.'[21] The banquet at which Love serves personally is not that of the earthly church, but that final 'communion' mentioned in Luke 12 :37, of which the present Communion is but an anticipation : 'Blessed are those seruants, whom the Lord when he commeth, shall find watching : Verily, I say vnto you, That he shall girde himselfe, and make them to sit downe to meate, and will come foorth and serue them.' However we read it the poem is moving, but it gains immensely in richness when we recognize the relationships it establishes between this world and the next, between abstracted and incarnate Love.

Within most of the individual poems the emphasis is on construction rather than pilgrimage. Herbert's imagery characteristically concerns the creator and the architect rather than the 'nests' and 'tears' of Crashaw; the 'light' of Vaughan, or Donne's imagery of death. God is specifically the *Architect* in

'The Church-floore', and He is almost everywhere the builder or the artist or the musician. One of the most convincing arguments against despair derives from the nature of God as artist: 'As Creatures, he must needs love them; for no perfect Artist ever yet hated his owne worke.'[22] Herbert rings all the traditional changes on 'stone' as the chief architectural element, under its various guises as the heart of man, the tomb of Christ, the law of Moses, 'the stone that the builders rejected'. The hardness of the stone was generally recognized; it was the employment of that hardness in the construction of a true temple which appealed to Herbert's imagination.[23]

In 'The World', 'Love's' work is to build a 'stately house'. 'Fortune' attempts to disguise the house's structure; 'Pleasure' ornaments it with *'Balcones, Terraces*, Till she had weakned all by alteration'; 'Sinne' 'The inward walls and sommers cleft and tore'; and 'Sinne' and 'Death' combined 'raze the building to the very floore';

> But *Love* and *Grace* took *Gloric* by the hand,
> And built a braver Palace then before.

In 'Vanitie (1)' the activities of the 'fleet Astronomer', the 'nimble Diver' and the 'subtil Chymick', divorced from the search for God, are the search for death; life is found in the discovery of God, and creation is its mark. In 'Deniall' separation from God is compared with the 'breaking' of a bow, of music, of a blossom, of the heart – and of rhyme and stanzaic structure.

There was for Herbert no one architectural pattern; there were almost as many patterns as there were experiences. But Herbert could not conceive of such a thing as a formless poem. 'The Collar', one of his most popular poems today, makes an immediate appeal to many readers with its expression of revolt and with what appears to be its daring use of 'free verse'. But the poem is not written in 'vers libres'; it is one of Herbert's most deliberate ventures in 'hieroglyphic form'. The object of imitation is the disordered life of self-will which rebels against the will of God and therefore lacks the order and harmony of art as well as of the religious life : a strict 'imitation' would be no form at all – and no poem at all. Herbert has given a formalized picture of chaos.

I struck the board, and cry'd, No more.
I will abroad.
What? shall I ever sigh and pine?
My lines and life are free; free as the rode,
Loose as the winde, as large as store.
Shall I be still in suit?
Have I no harvest but a thorn
To let me bloud, and not restore
What I have lost with cordiall fruit?
Sure there was wine
Before my sighs did drie it : there was corn
Before my tears did drown it.
Is the yeare onely lost to me?
Have I no bayes to crown it?
No flowers, no garlands gay? all blasted?
All wasted?
Not so, my heart : but there is fruit,
And thou hast hands.
Recover all thy sigh-blown age
On double pleasures : leave thy cold dispute
Of what is fit, and not. Forsake thy cage,
Thy rope of sands,
Which pettie thoughts have made, and made to thee
Good cable, to enforce and draw,
And be thy law,
While thou didst wink and wouldst not see
Away; take heed :
I will abroad.
Call in thy deaths head there : tie up thy fears.

He that forbears
To suit and serve his need,
Deserves his load.
But as I rav'd and grew more fierce and wilde
At every word,
Me thoughts I heard one calling, *Child!*
And I reply'd, *My Lord.*

For readers accustomed to a different tradition in poetry, the picture of chaos may not at first be apparent. Except for some permissible extravagance of emotion and certain ideas which prove fallacious from the point of view of Christian doctrine, there is in the thought no obvious indication of the failure of rational control. The poem is clearly divided into four sections of argument : the original complaint of the heart, the answering assurance of the will that there is 'fruit' if the heart would seek it, the repeated complaint and statement of purpose by the heart, and the final resolution. The heart originally rebels because of lack of 'fruit', and, as Helen White has noted,[24] after the early 'flowers' and 'garlands' the imagery becomes more vulgar as the emotion becomes 'more fierce and wilde'. But the meaning of Herbert's poem, his evaluation of that revolt and its resolution, is clearly imaged in the elaborate anarchy of the patterns of measure and rhyme. The poem contains all the elements of order in violent disorder. No line is unrhymed (a few rhymes occur as often as four times) and each line contains two, three, four or five poetic feet. (Herbert counted syllables. All the lines have four, six, eight or ten syllables except lines 12 and 14, with their conventional feminine rhymes, and lines 15 and 16, with their daring but still 'permissible' combination of short feet and feminine rhymes.) Although readers accustomed to Renaissance poetry might feel uncomfortable with the disorder of the first thirty-two lines, they could hardly divine the stanzaic norm which is the measure for that disorder until it is established, simultaneously with the submission of the rebel, in the final quatrain: 10^a 4^b 8^a 6^b. That pattern of line lengths and rhyme does not occur until the final four lines; before those lines the elements of the pattern are arranged so as to form almost the mathematical ultimate in lack of periodicy. If we consider that the first thirty-two lines represent eight quatrains, we discover six different patterns of rhyme (the only repeated one is the unformed *a b c d*) and seven patterns of line lengths. Until the final four lines, the poem dramatizes expertly and convincingly the revolt of the heart, and its imitation of colloquial speech almost convinces us of the justice of the cause. But the disorder of the poem provides a constant implicit criticism, and with the final lines we recognize that 'The Collar' is a narrative in past tense: the message for the present concerns the necessity of order.

The Temple is almost a casebook of examples showing how 'Order' gives 'all things their set forms and houres'.[25] It reflects Herbert's belief that form was that principle by which the spiritual created existence out of chaos, and Herbert assumed that that process could be rationally apprehended. Since the principle was divine and therefore universal, the understanding of the formal organization of any one object or state or action gave a clue to the understanding of the rest. The poet's duty was to perceive and to communicate God's form. In the process he would construct out of the chaos of experience and the mass of language another object which would reflect his discovery: literary form as we understand it was but a reflection of that form which was everywhere present, although often hidden to eyes that could not 'see'. It, too, in its material embodiment appealed to man's senses and moved his affections. The rational contemplation of it should lead to an understanding of its symbolic significance.

Such an undeviating effort to answer the question, 'How are all things neat?'[26] ran the risk of over-neatness. For a person who did not scrutinize the heart, who attempted to formulate the answers before he had experienced them, such an external conception of the function of the priest and the poet would leave the craftsman and the logician admirably free, but it might also lead to triviality and inhumanity. That Herbert was deflected so rarely from the genuine was the result not only of his integrity as man and as artist, but also of the nature and depth of his experienced suffering. Suffering, both spiritual and physical was the continuous challenge to the meaning of Herbert's existence and his art. Herbert believed that the Christian's life should be ordered in accordance with the will of God. As Austin Warren has remarked, the 'marks' of that order were joy and 'fruit' and peace.[27] When these were absent, a searching of the self and a passionate attempt at resolution were necessities. To Herbert it was not enough to present 'honestly' the ugliness and the disorder either in the worship of God or in poetry. That desperate sorrow which seemed meaningless and for which no resolution could be conceived could serve neither for worship nor for edification. But poetry was not therefore to be left to the secular 'lover's lute'.[28] Suffering for which some resolution or evaluation could be envisaged was the subject of the most moving poetry. While Herbert had experienced the joy and peace of resolution, he had also experienced its momentariness. He knew that the Christian's and the poet's forms were only approximations within time which had constantly to be renewed. The composition of the poems, imitative as they were of that ordering which he had experienced and which he hoped to experience again, was the act of the craftsman who shapes the imperfect materials of his own suffering as well as joy into a pattern symbolic of the divine order.

S o u r c e : *George Herbert. His Religion and Art* (1954).

NOTES

1. See Kenneth B. Murdock's discussion in *Literature &
Theology in Colonial New England*, pp. 8–29. I owe a great deal
to his comments on Herbert (Cambridge, Mass., 1949) pp. 21–7.
2. *Spiritual Exercises*, ed. Orby Shipley (London, 1870) p. 24.
3. *Lives*, ed. G. Saintsbury (London, 1927) p. 278.
4. *Ferrar Papers*, ed. B. Blackstone (Cambridge, 1938) p. 34.
For the symbolic design of the chapel at Little Gidding, see p. 28.
5. *Lives*, p. 301.
6. *L'Esthétique de Saint Augustin et ses sources* (Brno, 1933)
p. 199. I am reminded of Paul Oskar Kristeller's admonition concerning the historical impropriety of the word 'aesthetic' in such a
context. In their use of the word, however, Svoboda, and Katherine
E. Gilbert and Helmut Kuhn in *A History of Esthetics* (New York,
1939) pp. 129–30, 155–60, are conscious of Baumgarten's invention
of 1750 and of the fact that 'art' meant something quite different to
the ancients and the men of the Middle Ages from what it usually
means today. Yet thinkers before the Renaissance were immensely
concerned with the definition and the meaning of 'beauty', and their
conceptions of beauty, while never confined to the productions of
men's hands, were relevant to such productions. If we clearly understand the modernity of the ideas of an isolated group of 'fine arts'
and a particular 'psychology of the artist', the use of the word
'aesthetic' in itself should cause no misconceptions.
7. Augustine, *The Confessions*, tr. Pusey, Bk x, Chap. xxxiv.
8. Cf. Herbert's 'Sinne (II)'.
9. *Confessions*, Bk x, Chap. xxxiii
10. *The Anatomy of Melancholy*, ed. Floyd Dell and Paul Jordan-
Smith (New York, 1938) p. 95. Burton's quotation is hardly fair:
in *The Confessions*, Bk I, Chap. xvi, Augustine was condemning
the teaching of erotic pagan poetry to the young.
11. Herbert, 'The Pulley'.
12. *Of the Laws of Ecclesiastical Polity*, Bk v, Sect. lviii.
13. 'George Herbert and the Emblem Books', *Review of English
Studies*, xvii, 151.
14. See, e.g., the sections of Byrd's 'Magnificat' and Morley's

'Out of the Deep' printed in Edmund H. Fellowes's *English Cathedral Music from Edward VI to Edward VII* (London, 1941) pp. 77, 84.

15. Walton, *Lives*, p. 314.

16. Sermon x, 9 April, 1615, from *Ninety-Six Sermons, Works,* II (Oxford, 1841–54) 347–8. The entire sermon provides an interesting analogue to Herbert's thought.

17. *The Metaphysical Poets* (New York, 1936) pp. 167–8.

18. Hutchinson, *Works*, 2nd ed. (Oxford, 1945) pp. lv–lvi, summarizes the changes in order : 'the first sixteen poems in *W* are in nearly the same order as in *B*, but . . . after them there are only nine instances of two poems in the same consecutive order in *W* and *B*, until the group of nine *W* poems at the end of *B*. There are no *W* poems in *B* between No. 79, "Obedience" and the final group beginning with No. 156, "The Elixir" '. See Hutchinson's listing of the poems in *W* and his general discussion, pp. liii-lv, lxx-lxxiv.

19. The sequence of poems which I discuss is found in *Works*, pp. 44–61.

20. 'George Herbert', *Spectator*, CXLVIII, 360–1.

21. 'The Temple explained and improved', Bodleian, MS. Rawlinson D 199, p. 376.

22. *A Priest to the Temple, Works*, p. 283.

23. See 'Sepulchre'.

24. *The Metaphysical Poets*, p. 183.

25. 'The Familie'.

26. 'Man'.

27. *Rage for Order* (Chicago, 1948) p. 30.

28. See Herbert's 'Grief'.

Josephine Miles and Hanan C. Selvin

A FACTOR ANALYSIS OF THE VOCABULARY OF POETRY IN THE SEVENTEENTH CENTURY (1966)

Because, as Kenneth Burke and many other critics have suggested, the clustering of terms is important for verbal and literary style, the use of the mathematics of factor analysis seems a possible way of getting at clusters not evident to the reading eye, yet underlying whole modes of expression. Professor Hanan C. Selvin, now of the University of Rochester, has worked out procedures for testing this belief, using a program written by Professor Alan B. Wilson of the Department of Education at Berkeley; and our results, however tentative and exploratory, may be of interest to those concerned with the study of literary style.

The question we asked is whether the main words of reference used by the poets of the seventeenth century tend to be grouped into clusters of use, so that one is more, or less, predictable in terms of another. And the further question is whether in the use of these words the poets also cluster in groups in ways familiar or unfamiliar to literary generalization. These are, in other words, two parts of a question about poetic style in the seventeenth century.

To put it more technically : will a factor analysis of the sixty nouns, adjectives and verbs used at least ten times in a consecutive thousand lines by each of at least three of thirty poets in the seventeenth century reveal a number of factors useful for characterizing certain groups of poets and poetic habits of style? The representativeness of the thousand lines rests on the judgement that they provide a text long enough to show the poet's characteristic recurrences of word-use. For many poets, a thousand lines constitute their complete work. The stipulation of at least three poets aims to emphasize common uses rather than individual ones.

Factor analysis is a statistical procedure for measuring the extent to which groups of words have similar patterns of high and low use by various poets. In this paper, we shall speak of the words that make high contributions to a factor as forming a cluster. The reader should note that what Robert C. Tryon calls 'cluster analysis' is a different, though related, procedure.

Our basic data are frequencies of word-use. These frequencies can conveniently be shown in a 'score-matrix', table 1.

The figure '3' in the upper left-hand corner means that Jonson used the word *bright* three times in the thousand lines of *Underwoods*, his chief collection of poems. The blanks represent minimal or no uses. *Good* is the adjective Jonson uses most, sixteen times in a thousand lines. We take about ten times in a thousand lines, or a range from seven to twelve, as strong use; so Jonson can be seen to use five adjectives this strongly. Donne is quite similar in use of adjectives in general. Wither shares not at all in the use of these common adjectives, while Waller on the other hand is strongest in number and frequency of adjectives used, agreeing especially with Quarles, Shirley and Milton. If we read the excerpt in columns down rather than across, that is, consider the vertical rather than the horizontal lines as pairs, we may note that some words, like *good* and *great*, are used strongly by almost every poet, especially in Waller's time. Others, like *poor* and *bright*, seem almost mutually exclusive, or like *poor* and *true*, selectively related.

TABLE I

	60 major words: adjectives, nouns and verbs in alphabetical order. Here, the 11 adjectives:										
30 17th-century poets in chronological order	bright	fair	good	great	happy	high	new	old	poor	sweet	true
Jonson b. 1573	3	3	16	12		3	3	3	8	8	10
Donne 1576		5	20	6			15	6	7	5	20
Sandys 1578	2	14	2	12		7		5		8	
Fletcher 1582		19	15	25	10	8	11	7		6	
Wither 1588			10	10							10
Herrick 1591		6	14	4					6	17	7
Quarles 1592		13	25	10		5	13	5	18	8	8
Herbert 1593			10	20		6	4	3	6	6	5
Carew 1595	5	20	6	4						8	5
Shirley 1596	2	15	12	15			9	5	5		6
Waller 1606	12	30	15	20	5	10	10	7		12	5
Milton 1608	5	8	7	8	3	13	5	7		12	2
Suckling 1609		7	20	16			8				
Cleveland 1613			4	8	4			8		9	
Crashaw 1613	15	33	7	20		7	15	10	14	16	7

TABLE I (cont.)

30 17th-century poets in chronological order

60 major words: adjectives, nouns and verbs in alphabetical order. Here, the 11 adjectives:

	bright	fair	good	great	happy	high	new	old	poor	sweet	true
More 1614	7	10	30	25	8	6	6	9		7	6
Denham 1615		3	12	22	6	5	5	20		1	5
Cowley 1618	5	20	4	15	7					2	5
Lovelace 1618	15	14	7	4	7		7		7	6	7
Marvell 1621	5	10		10			5	2		17	15
Vaughan 1622	5	10									
Dryden 1631			5	16	5		7	4	11	1	8
Roscommon 1633			13	12	4		8	6			
Oldham 1653			10	21			9	12	7		7
Blackmore 1655	8		7	16	7	10					
Creech 1659			13	19	5	7	10	9			6
Garth 1661				20			9	7			
Walsh 1663	9	7	7	12	12		7				9
Prior 1664	9	9	5	26							
Pomfret 1667	8	7		12	8						9

So much one can see at a glance. But when the full matrix of thirty poets and sixty main adjectives, nouns and verbs is set up, the complexity is too great to be grasped in this way. It is difficult to look at sixty pairs of numbers and to estimate how closely one set resembles the other. The 'coefficient of correlation' is a much better tool for this purpose than is simple inspection. And it is even more difficult to grasp the complexity of 435 possible pairs of poets, when each poet is paired with every other poet. The statistical procedure known as factor analysis is an efficient tool for reducing such complexity to a simple form, and, thanks to the computer, it is also economical. The calculations reported here took between one and two minutes on a large computer; they would have taken months on a desk calculator, years with pencil and paper. Factor analysis asks whether thirty poets really represent thirty distinct forms of behavior or whether they might be more fruitfully considered as representing a smaller number of more general patterns of word-use.

Table 1, therefore, leads to two distinct but related lines of analysis: a study of the major patterns of word-use (the 'word-factors'), and a study of major patterns of poetic practice ('poet-factors'). The starting point for the study of poet-practice is the extent to which each pair of poets agree on use of terms – that is the extent to which each pair of horizontal lines is the same. Likewise, the starting point for the study of word-use is the extent to which each pair of words tends to be used together – that is, the extent to which each pair of columns is the same. The similarity is measured by the 'coefficient of correlation', which approaches 1.0 as the two columns become more nearly alike and −1.0 as they become more different. A zero correlation means that the two columns show no systematic relation; in this case, knowing that one member of the pair is used frequently by some poet tells nothing whatever about the frequency with which he uses the other member of the pair.

TABLE 2: POET-FACTORS

	Poets in chronological order	Factors: Correlation of poets with poet clusters				
		1	2	3	4	5
1	Jonson	.53	.48	.32	.11	−.35
2	Donne	.91	−.01	.13	−.05	−.10
3	Sandys	.53	.25	.20	.33	.44
4	Fletcher	.47	.27	.11	.38	−.05
5	Wither	−.07	−.08	.02	−.02	.25
6	Herrick	.63	.13	.36	.05	−.35
7	Quarles	.30	.34	.41	.35	−.08
8	Herbert	.35	.43	−.02	.17	.25
9	Carew	.86	.01	.18	.05	.11
10	Shirley	.70	.23	.31	.30	−.04
11	Waller	.59	.27	.19	.48	.10
12	Milton	.00	.02	.15	.71	−.03
13	Suckling	.75	.21	.26	−.08	−.34
14	Cleveland	.55	.03	.34	.00	−.14
15	Crashaw	.23	.19	.48	.65	.03
16	More	.30	.57	.15	.23	−.11
17	Denham	.49	.60	.12	.19	−.16
18	Cowley	.38	.38	.56	.05	−.18
19	Lovelace	.15	−.01	.66	.26	.14
20	Marvell	.09	.14	.54	.09	−.21
21	Vaughan	.04	−.27	−.24	.37	−.05
22	Dryden	.31	.60	.03	.03	.15
23	Roscommon	.06	.77	.17	−.12	.02
24	Oldham	.06	.76	.18	.14	−.29
25	Blackmore	.02	.70	.06	.05	−.07
26	Creech	−.00	.73	.07	.07	−.36
27	Garth	.80	.08	−.13	.09	.05
28	Walsh	.07	.24	.65	−.00	.21
29	Prior	.60	.21	−.27	.32	.04
30	Pomfret	.02	.56	.38	−.15	.16

Tables 2 and 3 represent the results of these two basic procedures; technically, they are the outcomes of 'varimax rotation of principal-axis factor extractions'. Note that, like table 1, table 3 is merely illustrative, not complete, showing just eleven adjectives of the sixty main words; that is, because of limits of space, just the top left-hand corner of a table which presents in its entirety thirty poets and sixty terms. The partial tables show how the factor-matrix can be used; complete tables are of course the basis for the fuller generalizations made here.

In table 2, which is complete, note that Jonson, as we might have concluded by reading the matrix table 1, is fairly moderate in his participation, looming large in no factor. Then note the very high number .91 for Donne in Factor 1. This means that Donne's word-usage has a great deal in common with that of every poet who has a high correlation with this factor – especially with Carew and Shirley for example, and least with Herbert, Wither and Milton. Factor 1 could well be called the Donne factor then, inasmuch as his practice defines it so fully, and his choices are so little a part of any of the other four factors. Factors 2 and 3 are less identifiable with one poet's emphases, but seem relative to certain groups: Factor 2 : Jonson, Quarles, Herbert; Factor 3 : Jonson, Quarles, Herrick, Shirley. Factor 4 is clearly Milton's, shared especially by Sandys, Fletcher, Quarles and Waller. Factor 5 is Sandys's with Jonson, Herrick and others in negative correlation, least apt to agree with Sandys. Participation in further Factors 6, 7 and so on, not shown, is so meager as to be marginal. In sum, the numbers in the table, the factor 'loadings', show the degree to which each poet, in terms of his frequencies in choice of certain words resembles the group which makes similar choices.

The numbers in excerpted table 3, on the other hand, show the degree to which each word, in terms of its use by all the poets, appears in a text in company with the other words. The first

TABLE 3: EXCERPT FROM WORD-FACTOR MATRIX

Words:
11 adjectives in
alphabetical order

*Factors: correlations of individual words
with word-clusters*

	I	II	III	IV	V	VI	VII
bright	−.15	−.20	.79	.07	−.09	−.05	.03
fair	.08	.17	.84	.04	−.04	−.03	.04
good	.33	.41	−.05	.03	.07	−.05	.29
great	.12	.13	.19	−.31	.15	.26	.71
happy	−.12	−.27	.18	.33	−.10	−.12	.67
high	−.16	.08	.24	−.20	.27	.19	.13
new	.16	.60	.18	−.07	−.10	−.16	.34
old	−.15	.30	−.30	−.36	.31	−.26	.26
poor	.01	.83	.22	.04	−.09	.10	−.20
sweet	−.05	.40	.49	−.08	−.19	−.02	−.39
true	−.07	.56	.08	.52	−.00	−.27	.07

column, Factor I, is closest to being identifiable by the word *good*; however, it is not vividly definable by any one adjective, but rather by its many strongly correlated verbs. Factor II, on the other hand, appears to represent that *poor* which we were able to discern in the matrix; now its relation comes clearer to other terms, not only to *true*, but also to *good, new, sweet.* In Factor III, the high correlation of *bright* and *fair* is most apparent. For Factor IV *true* is strongest; V and VI are mixed; and VII stresses *great* and *happy*, in contrast to *poor* and *sweet.*

Reading across the rows, note that for some words their appearance in certain contexts strongly defines them: *fair* in II and III, like *poor* and *sweet*, for example; *good* in I and II; *great* in VI and VII; *new* in II and VII; *true* in II and IV. Strong use thus seems to be limited to one or two chief clusters of use. The relation of *new* to *old* is particularly interesting: quite close in three factors, but with *new* dominating in II and III, subordinate in IV and V. By such clues we may gain insights into wider poetic views.

With these sections of the larger tables in mind, we may now summarize the data for the two factor-analyses, for poets and for words, and then we may look at the relation between them; that is try to render the matrix, by way of the factoring, into some generalization about seventeenth-century language in poetry. When we look at the groupings of poets in terms of the groupings of the sixty words they most use, the factors help us recognize more about these relations. The poets' Factor 1 associates almost half of the poets in a group in which Donne's uses are clearly dominant: Donne .91, Carew .86, Suckling .75, Shirley .70, Herrick .63, Prior .60, Waller .59, Cleveland .55, Jonson .53, Sandys .53, Denham .49, Fletcher .47, The so-called 'sons of Ben' turn out to be even more strongly sons of Donne. Factor 2 shows other sons of Ben, in a different light: increasing classicism and its chronological source in him: Roscommon .77, Oldham .76, Creech .73, Blackmore .70, Denham .60, Dryden .60, More .57, Pomfret .56, Jonson .48, Herbert .43.

The other, smaller groups of mid-century are: Factor 3, Lovelace .66, Walsh .65, Cowley .56, Marvell .54, Crashaw .48, Quarles .41; Factor 4, Milton .71, Crashaw .65, Waller .48; and Factor 5, the Sandys factor, 44 – to which there is strong negative correlation for non-Sandysian Jonson, Herrick, Suckling, and Creech.

For the larger number of words, a larger number of factors, seven, seem statistically and substantially important. Note that when the adjectives we have seen in table 3 are seen in relation with nouns and verbs, only three or four carry weight, and these for only two or three factors. Factor 1 for words shows the following high degrees to which each word participates in and accounts for the whole factor: *bring* .94, *lie* .94, *world* .90, *go* .89, *time* .86, *thing, find, give* .85, *love* .71, *death* .68, *make* .51.

While on the face of it this list may not seem to reveal a meaningful homogeneity, it is, in fact, remarkably packed with verbs of action, and with a world-time-love-death – reciprocal-action complex which we may recognize as part of what has often been called 'metaphysical'. These terms together bear a very high proportion of the whole burden of metaphysical vocabulary. The key terms of Factor ɪɪ are *poor* .83, *keep* .74, *come* .71, *make* .61, *new* .60, *true* .56, *day* .56, *know* .55; though also active these are yet more adjectival and normative than the metaphysical. The adjective relations are visible in excerpted table 3, as for Factor ɪɪɪ also.

The third factor: *fair* .84, *bright* .79, *eye* .74, *heaven* .70 – aesthetic, sensory with sublime associations. The fourth, emotional: *soul* .75, *love* .72, *fear* .69, *die* 64, *true* .52 – a different interrelating of concepts; like Factor ɪ, closely related to the vocabulary of the metaphysicals.

Factor v : four nouns, *god(s)* .81, *king* .76, *friend* .61, *power* .61. These appear to resemble or supplement Factor ɪɪɪ. Factor vɪ with its substantive *earth* .68, *sun* .63, *sin* .61, *life* .59, *light* .56, *sea* .58, may, like Factor ɪɪ, resemble and supplement the *great* .71, *happy* .67, *muse* .64, *art* .51, and *hear* .52 of Factor vɪɪ.

We have seen how highly Donne's uses account for Poet-Factor ɪ, and may note, inasmuch as the first factor accounts for most, in Word-Factor ɪ at least half of the terms are strong for Donne, especially *death, thing, world, find, give, love, make.* His *sun, thing* and *keep* are characteristic of earlier colleagues as *world* is of later ones. Jonson leads and exceeds Donne in the use of *great, god, life, light, man, nature, sin, call, fly, grow, hear, know, see*; and of these, many are used especially frequently by one or another of the later so-called 'classical' poets like Waller, Denham, Dryden, Oldham, Creech, Garth and Prior : while some, especially *great, sin, god* and *life,* are also peculiarly characteristic of Sandys and Herbert as distinguished from the other religious poets.

What the mid-group of Lovelace–Cowley–Marvell–Crashaw–Quarles–Walsh especially shares is the aesthetics of *bright, fair, poor, sweet, day, eye, fire, heaven, world* and the verbs *find, keep, know, make, see* – the adjectives, even the metaphors as in *fire*, of a more domesticated metaphysics. This was their carrying on and modifying of the Donne tradition.

What the Milton–Crashaw–Waller group shares especially is its use of *high, new, old, sweet, god, heaven, night, come, give, hear, make* – plus the Sandys factor combining *fair, earth, joy, night, soul*; with *joy* as strong only in Lovelace and Pomfret, with traces in Milton and Herbert; with *earth* as strong only in Prior; and with *soul* as strong also in Milton and Pomfret – a clearly Biblical grouping in addition to the more specially Miltonic, of which it seems a part.

We may discern then a sequence of both kind and degree. Most pervasive throughout the century is the Donnic temporal and emotional, neo-Platonic, world of love and death. Next is Jonson's Aristotelean life and nature of norms, less personal and active, more abstract and evaluative than Donne's and thus including *sin*, as do Herbert and Crashaw who work apart from the Donne tradition. Classical nouns of value increase during the century, until they appear most strong in the satiric and descriptive work of the neoclassicists from Dryden on.

Next are the two mid-groups, both sensory and aesthetic, the one more classical earthly, the other more Biblical heavenly, with appreciative adjectives and receptive verbs, with either *seeing* and *bright day* or *hearing* and *high night*, and the beginnings, in Sandy's, of the cosmology of *earth* as distinguished from *world*.

The main poetic lines therefore seem to comprise : pervasive, speculative, cognitive and active, Poet-Factor I and Word-Factors I and IV; an early and late normative and ethical, Poet-Factor 2 and Word-Factors II, VI and VII; a middle aesthetic both human and heavenly, Poet-Factors 3, 4 and 5 and Word-Factors III, V. The interweaving is strong, but the three major sources in reading, in Scholastic Petrarch, the Classics and the Bible are vividly clear, as well as the main progressions of the century away from its central metaphysical line toward the two others, human and sublime, which carry it into the next century.

Such lines we may note in the second stanza of Donne's 'Good-Morrow', in the words *good, soul, fear, love, make, new, world, go* and *show*.

> And now good morrow to our waking soules,
> Which watch not one another out of fear;
> For love, all love of other sights controules,
> And makes one little roome, an every where.
> Let sea-discoverers to new worlds have gone
> Let Maps to other, worlds on worlds have showne,
> Let us possesse one world, each hath one, and is one.

More classical in its generalizing terms of *love, muse, worth, thought, fate art, friend* is Jonson's *To Francis Beaumont*:

> How I do love thee, Beaumont, and thy Muse,
> That unto me dost such religion use!
> How I do fear myself, that am not worth
> The least indulgent thought thy pen drops forth!
> At once thou mak'st me happy, and unmak'st;
> And giving largely to me, more thou tak'st.
> What fate is mine, that so itself bereaves?
> What art is thine, that so thy friend deceives?
> When even there, where most thou praisest me,
> For writing better, I must envy thee.

And in *Lycidas*, the sensory *hearing*, on the *high* lawns of morning, after the fresh dews of *night*, the *bright* and risen star of *heaven*:

T.M.P.—G

Together both, ere the high Lawns appear'd
Under the op'ning eyelids of the morn,
We drove afield, and both together heard
What time the Gray-fly winds her sultry horn,
Batt'ning our flocks with the fresh dews of night,
Oft till the Star that rose, at Ev'ning, bright.
Toward Heaven's descent had sloped his westering wheel.

Certain emphases become more clear than we may often see them in critical histories: the primacy of the Donne tradition; the ethical allegiance of Herbert to Jonson; the early innovative force of Sandys and Quarles toward the Biblical aesthetic; and the isolation of Vaughan from his religious confrères, in contrast to the surprising general continuity in Prior and Pomfret.

Certain doubts may be raised. How representative of each poet is each studied work? How representative of poetic vocabulary are the sixty major words here studied? How useful are they to establish main strands of emphasis, when they are only matters of degree and each poet's choices are in total unique? All of these doubts are in a sense one; that is, they concern statements made about tendencies rather than about totals, and thus are not exhaustive. But within their accepted limits, I think that the statements not only make sense but show the possibilities for making sense beyond our normal capacity for perception. Given the specific texts listed for our thirty poets, given the sizable proportions of whole vocabulary which we know these major terms represent, and given certain traditions of agreement beyond the simple facts of literal quotation or borrowing, we may well be able to see to what degree poets share in a major terminology, and to what degree style rests in the content of recurrent reference. The strong appearance of certain factors, of certain terms like *world, poor* and *fair*, and of certain names like Donne's and Milton's, shows the force of both persons and concepts in the creation of an art.

There is also some question as to whether there are certain types of factors which persist from era to era. Factors which we may designate cognitive–active, normative–substantive and aesthetic–qualitative factors, stress certain parts of speech; if we make a similar analysis of twentieth-century terms, themselves so very different in content, so much more fully aesthetic than in the seventeenth century, we yet may note a similarity of contrasts. The *black* and *green* of one factor and the *leaf* and *tree* of another are highly sensory for Roethke, Eberhart and Lowell. They can be seen in contrast to the *wind* and *water*, the *blue, sea* and *sky* of two other factors close to Stevens, less concrete. Still abstracter are *bright, dark* and *move*, or *life, death, world, love, nothing*, or active *know, hear, die, go*, with *earth* and *day*, the Eliot factor.

Thus there seems to be a similarity of factorial structure in the work of poets in two centuries as different as the seventeenth and the twentieth, a similarity that appears even when the two sets of words used are apparently very different. This kind of underlying similarity may be seen in fields of study which appear to have even less in common. Charles Morris and others have suggested the stability of action, receptivity and judgement as factors. These are much the same as those found by Hanan Selvin in his study of qualities of leadership. Like modern artists, scholars may be pleased to find the lines of structure which run beneath the varied surface of art as of experience.

Here is the complete list of seventeenth-century works studied, with the complete list of sixty words emphasized (i.e., used about 10 times in the first 1000 lines) by at least three of them. Jonson, b. 1573: *Underwoods* (first 1000 lines). Donne, 1576: *Songs and Sonnets*. Sandys, 1578: *Song of Solomon, Jeremiah*. Fletcher, 1582: *Purple Island*. Wither, 1588: *Vox Pacifica*. Herrick, 1591: *Hesperides*. Quarles, 1592: *Shepherds Oracles*. Herbert, 1593: *The Church*. Carew, 1595: *Poems*. Shirley,

1596: *Poems.* Waller, 1606: *Poems.* Milton, 1608: *Nativity, L'Allegro, Il Penseroso, Lycidas, Comus.* Suckling, 1609: *Fragmenta Aurea.* Crashaw, 1613: *Steps to the Temple.* Cleveland, 1613: *Poems.* More, 1614: *Psychozoia Platonica.* Denham, 1615: *Cooper's Hill* (1668 edn). Cowley, 1618: *Mistress.* Lovelace, 1618: *Lucasta.* Marvell, 1621: *Poems* (through 'Coy Mistress'), *Appleton House.* Vaughan, 1622: *Silex Scintillans, Poems.* Dryden, 1631: *Absalom and Achitophel.* Earl of Roscommon, 1663: *Poems* (through 'Prospect'), *Horace's Art of Poetry.* Oldham, 1653: *Horace, Juvenal.* Blackmore, 1655: *Wit* (350 lines), *Nature* (500 lines), *Vanity, Happiness, Morning Thought.* Creech, 1659: *Odes . . . of Horace.* Garth, 1661: *Dispensary.* Walsh, 1663: *Poems.* Prior, 1664: *Poems on Several Occasions* (200 lines), *Solomon.* Pomfret, 1667: *Poems on Several Occasions – Choice, Death, Love Triumphant.*

Main words: bright, fair, good, great, happy, high, new, old, poor, sweet, true, art, blood, day, death, earth, eye, fear, fire, friend, god, heart, heaven, joy, king, life, light, love, man, muse, name, nature, night, part, power, sin, soul, sun, tear, thing, time, world, bring, call, come, die, find, fly, give, go, grow, hear, keep, know, lie, live, love, make, see. There are a few other main words, too many for the matrix, such as: seem, show, sing, stand, take, tell, think.

SOURCE: *The Computer and Literary Style* (1966).

Earl Miner

THE METAPHYSICAL MODE:
ALTERATION OF TIME (1969)

In some ways the most fascinating decade for poetry in the seventeenth century is the as yet insufficiently explored period from about 1645 to 1655. These ten years or so are a microcosm of the entire century, and no one poet writing at that time can be said to be wholly Metaphysical, Cavalier, Restoration or anything else. Always of course with the proviso that Milton is entirely himself. Henry Vaughan is especially useful among these poets, both because he is authentic in many poems as a poet and as a Metaphysical, and also because he shows how in the special circumstances of mid-century that kind of poetry was possible only by emphasizing certain tendencies that had been strongly present but not uppermost before. His death within five years of Dryden's should not obscure the fact that he was writing many of his poems even as Cowley was writing many of his. In fact, he began a few years before Marvell. But the poems he was writing at that time were Cavalier rather than Metaphysical, and he is probably the single important example of a poet who began in another style and then turned Metaphysical. (The reverse is common enough.) Herbert probably wrote secular poems that have not survived, but it is likely from what he says of his 'Jordan' poems that they were Metaphysical. Vaughan began with Cavalier poetry – lyrics and public poetry – buttressed by translations. The verse of his early stage appeared in the *Poems* of 1646 and was followed by the verse in *Olor Iscanus*, whose Dedication dates from 1647, although the volume did not appear until 1651.

It would have required great percipience in reading these volumes to foretell that Vaughan would become a major figure among Metaphysical poets. But just about this time he was busy on the poems in *Silex Scintillans*, which in 1650 preceded *Olor Iscanus* into print. The fluidity of poetic styles in the century is suggested by such dates and is confirmed by *Thalia Rediviva*, a collection Vaughan mentions as being in hand in 1673, though it was not published till 1678, when it appeared probably as a compilation of early and late poems by a hand other than the poet's. Often in this last volume we sense that elements from Metaphysical poetry combine with elements from Cavalier to produce one of the notes of Restoration poetry. We may take 'To Etesia parted from him, and looking back':

> Hath she no *Quiver*, but my Heart?
> Must all her Arrows hit that part?
> *Beauties like Heav'n, their Gifts should deal*
> *Not to destroy us, but to heal.*
> Strange *Art* of Love! that can make sound,
> And yet exasperates the wound;
> That *look* she lent to ease my heart,
> Hath pierc't it, and improv'd the smart.   (7–14)

Here we have the dialectic, conceits, wit, questions and exclamations we believe to be Metaphysical techniques. And so they are, but the poem has a social rather than a private tone – the italicized lines have not only the very cadence of a second-rate Restoration song but also the first person plural of the public world.

Like other major mid-century poets (Charles Cotton may be mentioned with Marvell, Cowley, Waller and others), Vaughan is Janus-faced, looking before and after. But there is also a true

Metaphysical vein in Vaughan's poetry, and a special realization in it of poetic tendencies begun much earlier. The often-quoted acknowledgment in the Preface to *Silex Scintillans* (2nd edn, 1655) suggests the direction to look: 'The first, that with any effectual success attempted a *diversion* of this foul and overflowing *stream* [of secular poetry], was the blessed man, Mr. *George Herbert*, whose holy *life* and *verse* gained many pious *Converts*, (of whom I am the least) . . .' There is much in Vaughan's best Metaphysical poetry that is owed ultimately less to Herbert than to Donne – splendid dramatic outbursts, a witty dialectic and certain kinds of concern with time. But the debt is owed directly to Herbert and, we observe, is expressed both in terms of 'holy *life*' and of '*verse*'. The combination of these two in poetry of course has its biographical implications, but the literary result is an approach primarily devotional. What I am suggesting is that Vaughan represents one version of the last phase of Metaphysical poetry and that this may be characterized, again in an adapted sense like my 'drama' and 'narrative', as 'meditation'.[1] The meditational approach sometimes has an element of drama, usually when it is a colloquy between man and God or Body and Soul. Sometimes it has concern with a place that is meditated on, or a time of meditation, or time as a subject to be transcended. But the dominant effort is toward a raising of musing and colloquy to exclamation or apostrophe, to that spiritual ecstasy which has led many people to speak of Metaphysical poetry, and especially that of Vaughan, as mystical. The meditative mode almost never sustains such flights and usually returns to drama or narrative in rather diffuse versions. But whereas Crashaw seems to have difficulty in touching earth, Vaughan struggles to stay in flight.

Such flights suggest what is certainly true, that like all else of importance in Metaphysical poetry, the *fons et origo* of meditation is to be found in Donne. At their best, his divine poems admit the maximum amount of meditation possible with drama. Both elements may be focused on time ('What if this present were the worlds last night'), on place ('At the round earths imagin'd corners, blow/Your trumpets, Angells') or on time and place both ('This is my playes last scene, here heavens appoint / My pilgrimages last mile'). Indeed time and place, with that wonderful immediacy of address of which Donne is master, combine to subsume a dominant dramatic cast. On a few occasions, the meditational mode does dominate in Donne. 'A Litanie' is a good example :

> Father of Heaven, and him, by whom
> It, and us for it, and all else, for us
> Thou madest, and govern'st ever, come
> And re-create mee, now growne ruinous :
> My heart is by dejection, clay,
> And by selfe-murder, red.
> From this red earth, O Father, purge away
> All vicious tinctures, that new fashioned
> I may rise up from death, before I'am dead.   (1–9)

There is here no sense of functioning time and place, and drama has turned to musing prayer, a combination of 'holy *life* and *verse*'.

Herbert, who is all but entirely a devotional poet, is of course more meditational (in my sense) than Donne. Herbert is, as we have seen, often dramatic, and his dramas often have narrative frames. But frequently Herbert is as fully meditational as any of the Metaphysicals; that is, he will be found speaking and thinking but not at a dramatic time and place or in a narrative sequence. This aspect of Herbert's poetry can be shown by a couple of stanzas from 'Grace' :

> My stock lies dead, and no increase
> Doth my dull husbandrie improve :
> O let thy graces without cease
>   Drop from above ! . . .

> The dew-doth ev'ry morning fall;
> And shall the dew out-strip thy Dove?
> The dew, for which grasse cannot call,
>   Drop from above.   (1–4; 9–12)

One cannot say that there is no drama here, or that such meditation in other poems excludes narration in the sense of strongly implied sequence. But it is a drama of prayer, not a drama enacted at a time or place. There is also something akin to drama in the constant pressure toward transcendence – of place to heaven, of time to eternity and of ordinary drama to union. Herbert's ability to do this is clear enough in many poems, but 'The Temper (1)' is especially useful for illustration and its possibilities for making discriminations:

> How should I praise thee, Lord! how should my rymes
>   Gladly engrave thy love in steel,
>   If what my soul doth feel sometimes,
>   My soul might ever feel!
>
> Although there were some fourtie heav'ns, or more,
>   Sometimes I peere above them all;
>   Sometimes I hardly reach a score,
>   Sometimes to hell I fall. . . .
>
> Whether I flie with angels, fall with dust,
>   Thy hands made both, and I am there:
>   Thy power and love, my love and trust
>   Make one place ev'ry where.   (1–8; 25–8)

The distinction between the dominant meditation here and dominant drama in Donne can be quickly understood by setting beside the last stanza four lines from Donne's 'Good-morrow':

> And now good morrow to our waking soules,
>   Which watch not one another out of feare;
> For love, all love of other sights controules,
>   And makes one little roome, an every where.   (8–11)

Donne's language is not more particular than Herbert's, and
the concluding concept is essentially the same. But there is this
difference that we feel and that evokes in us a very different
response: Donne's 'one little roome' is a chamber, a curtain-bed,
in which the two lovers awake and find in their joy that all they
desire is right there. It is, then, a specific, felt place at a specific,
felt time, and the urge to transcend rather transforms the time
and place than aspires for that which is beyond. Herbert is
thinking of some of God's attributes – omnipotence, immanence
and love – and it is not so much the speaker's one place and time
that is important as, so to speak, God's eternity and ubiquity. Both
share a rapture, but with Herbert it is Vaughan's meditative combination of 'holy *life*' ('How should I praise thee, Lord!') and
of '*verse*' ('my rymes').

What Herbert frequently does, Vaughan almost always tries
for in *Silex Scintillans*. He is uneven, as a meditative poet is apt
to be. He has very, very few poems that sustain their best effects;
but what is equally important, he has in this collection very, very
few poems that are untouched by his best meditative mode. He
seems far more aware of time and place than Crashaw, but because he is aware, he seeks to transcend them in flight, whether in
time or place or in occult musing. 'Childe-hood' treats a favorite
subject, and it might therefore be thought to provoke a thematic
use of time contrasting the present and the past. That is indeed
what the poem comes to, but it is not that with which it begins:

> I Cannot reach it; and my striving eye
> Dazles at it, as at eternity....
> Quickly would I make my path even.
> And by meer playing go to Heaven.
>
>   Why should men love
> A Wolf, more then a Lamb or Dove?
> Or choose hell-fire and brimstone streams
> Before bright stars, and Gods own beams? (1–2; 7–12)

It may seem that a passage like this one – so lacking in wit, conceits, strong lines and other ordinary criteria for defining Metaphysical poetry – is simply not Metaphysical. Of course the label is not as important as the poem. But I think that somewhat similar passages from an earlier and a later poem will suggest that in Vaughan's poem we do have something different, and that what is different is something that we may as well call Metaphysical, since it is to be found to a smaller or larger degree in poets usually given the name. In the sixth stanza of Milton's 'On the Morning of Christ's Nativity' (1621) we have stars as emblems of providence, as in Vaughan's poem, and a threat against that providence, also as in Vaughan :

> The Stars with deep amaze
> Stand fixt in steadfast gaze,
>   Bending one way their precious influence,
> And will not take their flight,
> For all the morning light,
>   Or Lucifer that often warn'd them thence ;
> But in their glimmering Orbs did glow,
> Until their Lord himself bespake, and bid them go.
>
>   (69–76)

The differences are remarkable. Vaughan's speaker is isolated in a retreat from a sorry world, musing on God's goodness to man. Milton (here at age twenty-one) shows an intimate familiarity with the larger reaches of the universe, and to his lyric gives an essentially heroic narrative. A different example may be found in the conclusion to Dryden's *Hind and the Panther* (1687) :

> For now the streaky light began to peep;
> And setting stars admonish'd both to sleep.
> The Dame withdrew, and, wishing to her Guest
> The peace of Heav'n, betook her self to rest.
> Ten thousand Angels on her slumbers waite
> With glorious Visions of her future state.   (III, 1293–8)

Here we have true narrative rooted in time and suggestive, with
divine providence, of eternity. There is no personal distress, but
rather a vision of the Catholic Church as bride of Christ : the
stars are part of the narrative scene (in an allusion to the *Aeneid*)
and by association link to their intelligences, the angels that post
divine guard. What Milton and Dryden do not possess is most
readily specified as the private mode, and particularly a privacy
suggesting a direct intimacy between the speaker and God, as
well as a privacy expressing a shrinking from the world. Only
apart from the world, only by oneself, may one muse, may one's
heart be lifted up in the silent call of prayer; and, to these poets,
only in such private musings was the surge of exaltation possible.

Everyone familiar with Metaphysical poetry is familiar with
Vaughan's breathtaking beginning of 'The World' : 'I Saw
Eternity the other night. . . .' This, which is thought the finest
part of the poem, shows time transcended by eternity, place by
the totality of the universe – in the musing of a private speaker.
The force of the musing is often augmented in Vaughan's
poetry by symbols – eternity is a ring and is suggested by light –
that have been variously called emblematic, Hermetic and otherwise. 'Cock-crowing' and 'The Waterfall' are often given as
examples of such thought. In fact, there was a very great rise
during the 1640s and the 1650s in numerous forms of occultism,
typology, perennial symbolism, 'natural magic' and suggestive
lore. Those who would deny such elements in Vaughan, and
those also who would insist that they *must* be called Hermetic,
should compare the opening of 'Cock-crowing' with the opening,
and the notes on the opening, of the first fable in John Ogilby,
The Fables of Aesop Paraphras'd in Verse, 1651 and several
times reprinted.[2] The point is that Vaughan's allegiance to the
Metaphysical race is not due to the 'mystical', 'occult', or 'Hermetic' lore he shared with numerous contemporaries but to his exploration of the meditative strain in Metaphysical poetry.

Almost always his poems rise and fall as he seeks to intensify his *'verse'* by meditations of a 'holy *life'*. Perhaps the best example of this mode is in one of his finest and most characteristic poems, 'They are all gone into the world of light!'

> They are all gone into the world of light!
> And I alone sit lingring here;
> Their very memory is fair and bright,
> And my sad thoughts doth clear. . . .
>
> I see them walking in an Air of glory,
> Whose light doth trample on my days :
> My days, which are at best but dull and hoary,
> Meer glimmering and decays. . . .
>
> Dear, beauteous death! the Jewel of the Just,
> Shining no where, but in the dark;
> What mysteries do lie beyond thy dust;
> Could man outlook that mark! . . .
>
> Either [, God,] disperse these mists, which blot and fill
> My perspective (still) as they pass,
> Or else remove me hence unto that hill,
> Where I shall need no glass.
>
> (1–4; 9–12; 17–20; 37–40)

As so often, in Metaphysical poetry, the musing takes on the quality of address, and the grammatical modes are more often than in most other styles the less ordinary: interrogative, imperative and vocative. Fourteen of the poems in *Silex Scintillans* begin with an 'O . . .' (Similarly, eighteen of Herbert's poems begin in such fashion; in all Dryden's canon, only three.) The impulse behind meditation, like its private character, is something shared with the other dominant structures – the dramatic and the narrative. The meditative does not create the intense scene of the dramatic nor work as directively as the narrative, but it does seek intensity and movement. The effort toward transcendence is, then, a common motive in Metaphysical poetry, and the meditational structure hovers or muses over a subject until, or as long as, it proves capable of rapture. Obviously, this is the hardest structure to sustain, and Vaughan, who is the most given to meditation of all the major Metaphysical poets is, with Crashaw, the most uneven. 'The World' begins in glory, falls to sinful earth and rises at its end once more to glory. We do not much mind Vaughan's irregular falls when we come to know with full assurance that he will rise, and rise yet again. Indeed, as 'The World' and certain other of his poems show, he often incorporated dramatic and narrative elements into his meditational structure. Perhaps the real truth is that a given narrative structure by Vaughan is remembered for its meditative moments. In *Thalia Rediviva* there are some poems that are almost wholly meditational, and they are not nearly so satisfactory. This tendency toward meditation alone is to be found in its most advanced state in Traherne. Traherne has a few fine poems but none that one feels rise to greatness, and most of them are less effective than his prose-poetry. One would rather have a writer over-praised than undervalued. But with Traherne one main line of Metaphysical poetry was at its end. New experience, and new styles answering to that experience, had intervened. As Traherne shows, one could now be a Metaphysical only by an actual separation from the world. Donne, Herbert, Crashaw, Marvell and Vaughan very well knew the world they fled, and that is one reason why their private mode has the integrity and intensity it does. To be a Metaphysical poet as late as Traherne, one had to meditate alone, almost nowhere, almost at no time. Drama was past, and narrative was past. After musing there was silence – or the social voice and argument of 'almost the last of that race', Cowley.

Abraham Cowley has been as undervalued in our time as Traherne has been over-rated. It is true that in his famous review of 1921 T. S. Eliot said that Cowley ('at his best') possessed that sensibility which he found wanting in Milton and Dryden. Certainly Cowley is the best mid-century poet after Marvell, and is, in a few respects, not very far after. The two share a number of qualities, but in some ways Cowley is more like Donne than is Marvell. It will be recalled that in his *Life* of Cowley, Dr Johnson took examples of Metaphysical techniques and faults (there was not always a difference, to Dr Johnson's mind) almost equally from Cowley and Donne. But one is entitled to think both Dr Johnson and T. S. Eliot wrong, and there are perhaps not a few people who think that Cowley is in no meaningful sense a poet in 'the line of Donne'; and others that he is, but that his poems are inconsiderable. It is the first question to which I should like chiefly to address myself, because though it is no real answer to the second, the presence of Cowley in my discussion implies an estimate of his worth as a poet.

Cowley is sometimes more Cavalier or even more proto-Restoration than he is Metaphysical. His anacreontic verse follows Cavalier values, and his ode to the Royal Society fits Restoration values. Sometimes Cowley is wholly Metaphysical and not very poetic, or at least not very successful. Dr Johnson found the second stanza of 'The Innocent Ill' especially Metaphysical and especially bad :

> Though in thy Thoughts scarce any Tracks have been,
>   So much as of *Original* Sin,
>   Such Charms thy *Beauty* wears as might
> Desires in dying confest *Saints* excite.
>   Thou with strange *Adultery*
>   Dost in each breast a *Brothel keep*;
>   *Awake* all Men do *lust* for thee,
>   And some *enjoy* thee when they *sleep*.
> Ne'er before did *Woman* live,
> Who to such *Multitudes* did give
> The *Root* and *Cause* of *Sin*, but only *Eve*.

It would be difficult to frame a description of Metaphysical poetry that would include Donne's secular poems and exclude this stanza, as Dr Johnson unerringly recognized. But something has gone wrong. Donne is occasionally blasphemous and often outrageous. But his poems retain either a morality more basic than conventional moralism or leave us with the conviction that what they say is appropriate for such a speaker on such an occasion. Cowley's poem is obviously private. . . . But there is in this poem a lack of conviction, and it may be got at most readily in the terms of this chapter, formal procedures.

This seems the most revealing, as well as the most difficult, approach. Some of Cowley's poems are different, but the stanza just given is nonetheless symptomatic in lacking drama, narrative and meditation. Of those three, Cowley is most skillful with narrative, but the poems one is most readily inclined to call Metaphysical are often like the stanza from 'The Innocent Ill'. One feature, a negative one, is a tendency to abstraction implied by his very titles. Although *The Mistress* would be as good a title for Donne's *Songs and Sonnets* as for the collection of Cowley's most Metaphysical poems, individual titles are less happy : 'The Innocent Ill', 'The Soul', 'The Passions', 'Wisdom' and 'The Despair'. The abstraction seems to me a symptom of the removal from time and place in these poems. But if the poems neither cohere about a dramatic center nor develop along a narrative line, in what does their structural coherence lie? I think that it lies in what may be called 'argument'. As in Donne (and, it must be admitted, in Suckling) so in Cowley there is almost always a man addressing a woman or some other presumptive audience. The man and his audience are specifiable, even if their time and place are not. And the nature of the address is argument in the sense both of the dialectic . . . and of the pursuit with urgent show of language of whatever point the poem sets out to make. This explains why the woman herself innocent of any ill may keep a brothel in each breast, why she is a greater cause of sin to multitudes than any since Eve. What many people were formerly pleased to find in Donne is what I often find in Cowley: quaint hyperbole, and not so much of language and imagery, though of them certainly, as of thought. This is part of the argument, too, as if by calling a rise in the ground a mountain one may get agreement that it is a hill.

The exaggeration seems to me a symptom of a lack of conviction related to the absence of time and place coordinates in the poems. Too often Cowley does not know where such experience exists. He knows all the forms very well indeed, and the techniques lie ready to hand. But the woman, and the experience of love, have to be conjured into being by strong measures and held before the mind by a degree of argument louder than Donne or other Metaphysicals of stature equal to Cowley found necessary. What we see in Cowley is, I believe, what we see in other terms in Vaughan and Traherne. The private mode is growing more and more marginal. It had begun as a revulsion from the Elizabethan court and had found conviction either in anonymous urban privacy or in private prayer. Whatever the cause – the Civil Wars and the following strain of English life – by the middle of the century it was hard to keep a balance between the private world and the public. Nothing could better indicate Marvell's poise than just such an achievement (in separate poems). But writers like Vaughan were driven farther inward to isolation and musing, beyond even the private mode (Vaughan so often sounds a note as of one left behind), and that brooding is reflected in the very structure of their poems. Cowley, on the other hand, is torn between the public and the private worlds. And I believe that his Metaphysical poetry is a compromise between the two. It retains the private character and the wit of Metaphysical poetry, but it introduces a special social tone unknown before in Metaphysical poetry. The same vacillation between the active and the retired life will, of course, be found throughout the century. But it is less often found explicitly in poetry than in prose. (Marvell solved the problem by advocating the contemplative life in 'The Garden' and the active in the 'Horatian Ode'.) Cowley's essays, which possess an ease and quiet charm not always found in his poems, explicitly deal with the question, and they usually answer it by arguing the case for the retired life in the new social voice of the English Gentlemen (whose birth can almost be dated from those essays). Somewhat similarly, the argument of the poems has a strong social tone, because Cowley uses his hyperbole, at least as Eliot says, 'at his best', as a form of gently mocking humor. 'The Innocent Ill' is a kind of loudness no gentleman (in theory) could be guilty of. But the same tendency to argument, pursuing a point with a show of logic in talking with a woman, the same argument and the social tone, can be seen in a poem like 'Inconstancy':

> Five Years ago (says *Story*) I lov'd you,
> For which you call me most *Inconstant* now;
> Pardon me, Madam, you mistake the *Man*;
> For I am not the same that I was then ...
> My *Members* then the *Father Members* were,
> From whence *these* take their Birth, which now are here.
> If then this *Body* love what th'other did,
> 'Twere *Incest*; which by Nature is forbid.   (1-4; 11-14)

'Pardon me, Madame' – there is a note not heard before in Metaphysical poetry, though the disingenuous sly mockery *was* known to Suckling and other Cavaliers. The scientific premise of the poem and the sexual detail build up the argument around a single line of argument: inconstancy is change; I am changed; therefore I am not what I was; therefore I am not inconstant. What this poem also shows is that Cowley could be playful, invoking history ('*Story*', *storia*) with a light touch.

The more one reads Cowley, the more one is drawn into liking him, because one begins to detect a note of shyness or hesitation under the show of argument, and one begins to suspect that his poems are exaggeratedly fictional so that he can avoid seeming to talk about the subject that really interests him, himself. Again and again the argument directed toward the woman or other audience turns out to be a transparent way of talking about his sexual passion ('The Innocent Ill'), his own bewildering alterations ('Inconstancy') or, in a different tone, of his integrity ('All over Love'):

> Whatever *Parts* of me remain,
> Those *Parts* will still the *Love* of thee retain;
> For 'twas not only in my Heart,
> But like a *God* by pow'rful Art,
> 'Twas *all* in *all*, and *all* in *ev'ry Part*.
>
> *My'Affection* no more perish can
> Than the *First Matter* that compounds a Man.
> Herafter if one *Dust* of Me
> Mix'd with another's *Substance* be,
> 'Twill *leaven* that whole *Lump* with Love of Thee.
>
> (6–15)

In a sense not altogether different from its applicability to Donne's poems, the phrase 'dialogue of one' also applies to Cowley's approach. In Donne, however, there is such greater certainty as well as greater consciousness of the self that he can, in good faith, count his 'five gray haires' and think the number says something (allowing the requisite humor) about human experience. Cowley seems to find it necessary for either social of poetic convention to address 'The Mistress', perhaps because he lacks the conviction that his private experience is wholly valid.

Cowley's argument, like Vaughan's meditation, is, then, a means of discovery and of expression. But structurally the two

poets work in contrary terms. Vaughan meditates on a topic, rising and falling in flights of rapture. Cowley pursues a straight
line of argument, with the points of logic and the conceits mark-
ing stages of the journey. In this he resembles Donne much more
than do Vaughan and Traherne, as may be seen at once by a
comparison of Donne's 'Blossome' with Cowley's 'Welcome' to
his errant heart:

> Go, let the *fatted Calf* be kill'd;
>   My *Prodigal's* come home at last,
> With noble Resolutions fill'd,
>   And fill'd with Sorrow for the past.
> No more will burn with *Love* or *Wine*,
> But quite has left his *Women* and his Swine.
>
>   (1–6)

It is a pity that Cowley did not always write so directly about
himself (or a poetic speaker like himself). But there is another
vein in which his tendency to abstraction produced a kind of
poetry which is no doubt somewhat tenuous, yet which is also
possessed of real integrity. Both 'For Hope' and 'Against Hope'
are poems of that kind. And there are also his elegies, on Crashaw
and Hervey, that are among his finest poems. They are also
among his best known, and my aim has been to revive the lyric,
Metaphysical Cowley in whom we may discover one of the last
phases of the revolution begun by Donne. The manifesto of that
revolution had been an exploration or a dramatizing of time and
place as part of lyric experience, with meditation and argument
as means of sustaining the illusion that a speaker and audience
were present at that time and place. In poets following Donne,
narration comes to replace drama, and place gradually fades.
Except for Marvell, Metaphysical poetry in its last phase had
neither world enough nor time, and what was left was a sustaining of the private mode in meditation or in argument. Poets before Cowley and poets after him knew how to argue. Donne and

Dryden are masters of the art. Dryden does not concern us (much as there is of the Metaphysical in him), because the radically public nature of his poetry marks its division from the radically private nature of Metaphysical poetry. But it is obvious that argument is, in some sense, an element in a great deal of poetry from Donne to Cowley, and it is also obvious that argument somehow involves that wit which, from Dryden on, critics have associated with Metaphysical poetry.

S o u r c e : *The Metaphysical Mode from Donne to Cowley* (1969).

NOTES

1. Martz, Dame Helen Gardner in her edition, John Donne, *The Divine Poems* (Oxford, 1959) and others show how varieties of the formal religious meditation were drawn upon by different poets, both as general models and, at times, for formal division. My usage will be clear from the rest of the paragraph, but it obviously includes the technical as well as a more general application. As late as Traherne, formal religious meditations were being written. See *Meditations on the Six Days of the Creation*, ed. George Robert Guffey, Augustan Reprint Society, no. 119 (1966).

2. Ogilby treats the cock's seed, its ray, the hurt to lions and other old topics he discusses in terms both of the fabulists and the philosophers, particularly the Pythagoreans and Epicureans. Few subjects seem to me more in need of desimplification than the current one of scientific vs 'occult' thought in the seventeenth century. The evidence shows that Dryden's poetic and intellectual stand antedates in important ways Milton and Donne's (see, besides my *Dryden's Poetry* (Bloomington, 1967) ch. v and pp. 273–83, the numerological analysis by Alistair Fowler and Douglas Brooks, 'The Structure of Dryden's "Song for St. Cecilia's Day" ', *Essays in Criticism*, xvii [1967] 434–47). No discussion of the literary effects of science can afford omission of the extraordinary transformation of Samuel Butler's Sidrophel from interregnum astrologer

to virtuoso of the Royal Society; see *Hudibras*, Pt. ii, canto iii and the following 'An Heroical Epistle of Hudibras to Sidrophel'. Vaughan, Henry More, Dryden and, for that matter, Isaac Newton believing in astrology, secretly practicing alchemy while Master of the Mint and interpreting the prophecies of Daniel are much more like each other than one could guess from the usual attempts to make bogeyman and destroyers of 'sacramental' thought out of Bacon, Hobbes and the Royal Society.

Rosalie L. Colie

ANDREW MARVELL: STYLE AND STYLISTICS (1970)

The place conveniently assigned to Andrew Marvell among seventeenth-century poets may be a generalization for the convenience of teachers, but it is also true. He does sum up in his practice most of the major idiosyncratic styles of the period; his work provides traces of the major 'schools' of poetry into which late-Renaissance English verse is often divided. He shares something with the metaphysical school, with the classical school, and much with 'Miltonic' moral poetry. Marvell is a mediator in lyric style, as in much else: from the *concettismo* of Cleveland and Crashaw to the smoothness of Carew, from the understatement of Herbert to the brilliant emblematism of Vaughan, from the wit of Donne to the metaphysics of Traherne, examples may be found in Marvell's work. As in so many other literary areas, Marvell experimented with stylistic alternatives, and – miraculously – managed in spite of his eclecticism or his virtuosity, his mimicry or his imitativeness, to make a style of them recognizably his own. To the trained ear and eye, Marvell's poems cannot be confounded with the verse of any other of that mob of gentlemen that writ well.

Unquestionably, Marvell's experimentalism led him to play with language and syntax as he played with traditions, conventions and generic modes. From Mr Leishman's painstaking examination of Marvell's poetical habits, it is clear that he shared with his literate contemporaries, readers and writers, a common education in the modes and decorum of literary expression. . . .

In some very obvious ways, Marvell's language clearly 'belongs' with Jonson's, in Mr Winter's and Mr Trimpi's pious plain-style category;[1] in other ways, equally obvious, it does not. Marvell was given to test-situations, and he tested plain-style writing as he tested decorative and ornamental styles; he worked with images in all kinds of ways, intellectually as well as sensuously. In 'The Definition of Love', for instance, Marvell experiments with the intellectual working-out of imagery in the manner of Donne: he outdoes the geometric imagery of 'A Valediction: forbidding mourning', in his own poem more fully explored and consistently developed than in Donne's. He manages his argument in terms of remarkable 'logical' consequence, as Donne did in 'A Valediction: of weeping'. In other poems, he stretched that 'untruthful' decorative device, the pastoral hyperbole, beyond its customary bounds, as Mr Leishman's analogues show us; his games with pastoral are extraordinary, both in content and in style. His antipodeans, tortoises and hemispheres; his swelling houses and metamorphosing meadows are, perhaps, Clevelandisms, but if so, they are also explorations of the conceited style itself which not only outdo Cleveland's habitual talent, but also demonstrate how even an outrageous conceit can be used to integrate thematic elements of a poem. 'The Match' perhaps provides a better example of the conceited style than the imagery of 'Upon Appleton House'; there, the major image is extended to absurdity, and the poet is forced to 'save' himself by the abrupt simplicity of the last line.

Marvell's range is astonishing. At one end of the scale, the simplicities of such a line, from the 'Horatian Ode', occurring amid passages in the grand style

And, if we would speak true,
Much to the Man is due.

are the more moving because of the distant, formal, hyperbolical praise which it immediately follows, sums up and 'corrects'; at the other the beautifully elaborate 'petrarchan' language of 'The Fair Singer' reminds readers of the sheer loveliness of conventional decorative language. To dismiss that poem as 'merely' petrarchan is to do it serious injustice, for the middle stanza magnificently demonstrates the harmonizing conventionally introduced in the first stanza, as it twines the artificialities into a careful counterpoint ('dis-intangled', 'curled trammels of her hair', 'Slave', 'subtile Art invisibly can wreath / My Fetters'), only to resolve them all in the simplest involuntary act of life – 'the very Air I breath'. As genres were characteristically mixed in this author's work, so are styles. Sometimes language pulls one way and syntax another, as in the pastoral poems, where the plain style and syntax is set against the sense of whole pastoral 'myth' made in praise of artefaction and contrivance.

Marvell's ways with imagery vary, and so do his ways with syntax, by no means consistent or programmatic. Mr Leishman finds Marvell's inversions stilted, careless and unprofessional, many of them forced by the simple exigencies of rhyme. Marvell's solecisms of this sort (if that is what they are) are less obvious to me than to Mr Leishman, and furthermore, I find similar usage everywhere in seventeenth-century poetry. It was, I think, by Marvell's time, a little archaic to use 'do' and 'did' to fill out the metrics of a line, although vernacular usage still sanctions it. Marvell did go in for inversion, though not significantly more than his contemporaries. What is more important than this kind of habit, I think, is the question of obscurity in Marvell's syntax: there, it seems to me, he permitted himself more syntactical ambiguities than most of his contemporaries. Some of these ambiguities may be the result of his strong latinity; he learnt from

Ovid, from Virgil and especially from Horace to hinge two quite different phrases or clauses on a single word. Of this, more below : the trick is connected with Marvell's power to pun.

A glance at a few passages may show some of the anomalies in his practice. His tendency to epigram, for instance, naturally reinforces the tendency toward simple syntax :

> I sup above, and cannot stay
> To bait so long upon the way.

> A Soul that knowes not to presume
> Is Heaven's and its own perfume,

says the Resolved Soul, whom one would expect to speak plainly. The *style*, though, in which Created Pleasure speaks, is no more complex :

> Welcome the Creations Guest,
> Lord of Earth, and Heavens Heir.
> Lay aside that Warlike Crest,
> And of Nature's banquet share :
> Where the Souls of fruits and flow'rs
> Stand prepar'd to heighten yours.

Pleasure is in fact no less epigrammatic, no less plain, than the Soul is :

> Wilt thou all the Glory have
> That War or Peace commend?
> Half the World shall be thy Slave
> The other half thy Friend.

The linguistic difference between the two speakers in this dialogue lies not in their syntax, but in their imagery, their terms of argument. Pleasure offers 'Nature's banquet', 'the Souls of fruits and flow'rs', 'downy Pillows', 'charming Aires', and so forth, all elements which, even when so simply stated as this, inevitably call up affective sense-associations. Created Pleasure is an

Epicurean, but her sentence structure is stoically plain. In 'The Coronet', as often remarked, the wreathing, writhing, serpentine complexities of wordliness are expressed in an involuted, gordian syntax made sharply to contrast with the moralizings of the poem's final ten lines, these written in a direct and limpid syntax. In the involuted first sixteen lines, though, there are relatively few figures of speech which cannot in some sense be regarded as dictated by the poet's choice of fictional environment:

> When for the Thorns with which I long, too long,
>   With many a piercing wound,
>   My Saviours head have crown'd,
> I seek with Garlands to redress that Wrong:
>   Through every Garden, every Mead,
> I gather flow'rs (my fruits are only flow'rs)
>   Dismantling all the fragrant Towers
> That once adorn'd my Shepherdesses head.
> And now when I have summ'd up all my store,
>   Thinking (so I my self deceive)
>   So rich a Chaplet thence to weave
> As never yet the king of Glory wore:
>   Alas I find the Serpent old
>   That, twining in his speckled breast,
>   About the flow'rs disguis'd does fold,
>   With wreaths of Fame and Interest.

The poem is written from within the pastoral fiction, as if the poet were in fact a shepherd, in fact gathering flowers. He used to gather flowers to make garlands for his lady love, but now seeks them to make soothing, sacrificial garlands for his God. As he picks the flowers, he finds a snake: Eve, Eurydice, any child has had his experience. So far, everything in the poem is well within possible naturalistic experience, once one has accepted the limits of the pastoral mode. The 'pastoralism' is so natural, indeed, that the pastoral images are barely figurative; in this context, oddly enough, the *moral* statement seems the most figurative element – 'wreaths of Fame and Interest'.

The figures, then, are so naturalized within the pastoral as to lose their figurative power : the poet mocks their cliché quality by taking their fiction literally. Such 'unfiguring' and 'unmeta-phoring' characterizes much of Marvell's practice and is, I think, a function of his critical analysis. He turns back, as it were, to actualize the charged language of poetic traditions. In many ranges of his practice, Marvell tends to unfigure – to 'unpun', for instance, in a phrase like 'The *Nuns* smooth tongue has suckt her in'; or to literalize metaphor, as in the assumption in 'The Garden' that, plants being better than humans, the gods deliberately metamorphosed girls into laurel and rushes; or, to show the transfixing force of mourning and grief, to turn a be-reaved girl into a statue. Again and again, he pushes against the devices of his craft to find the literal truth they contain. He cleans them of their conventional metaphorical associations to begin anew. This trick manages at once to maintain the advantages of accrued traditional meaning, the literary 'charge' of the device, and to return us to the source of the figure, so that by apparently negating the figurative content, the poet actually enlivens what was so conventional as to be a cliché or near-cliché forcing the reader to take the conventional image seriously, to give a sharp look at an old custom. In terms of style, the process of unfiguring is very interesting : while it certainly seems to make style 'plainer' or 'straighter', it also points to the fact that pseudo-plainness, the 'poetry of statement', is in fact a form of figure, too, this time an intellectual figure. The area of fictionalization has been removed from the decorative or figurative level to the level of thought and theme. As the poet discusses his intentions in 'The Coronet' – to find appropriate flowers and to plait them into ap-propriate garlands – he makes his unmetaphored figure stand for something made out of metaphors, or makes his figure stand for the writing of poetry. Further, his 'garlands' signify the *paragone* between sacred and secular writing, which in its turn is made to stand for the struggle of soul and body, or for the contest between ways of life sacred and secular.

The first sixteen lines of 'The Coronet' are written in what Morris Croll has called the loose periodic Attic style : phrases and clauses are crossed and thwarted by other phrases and clauses, the principal verb so delayed as to make us unsure of the parts of speech in the first line. Does the poet also 'long' for thorns, or does he long for them for too long a time, or both? What does the verb 'seek' govern, 'for the Thorns' or 'to redress', or both? The sixteen lines are two sentences of eight lines each, both sharply broken up, wedged, and qualified by their various elements, to represent on the one hand a gradually unfolding experience which, as Croll has taught us, so much of the loose grammatical structure of the Attic prose seeks to impart; and on the other, to 'match' the grammar to the 'wreathing' of the subject. The experience itself is, first, one of recoil, of self-deception, of self-deception uncovered; the wreathing syntax can be seen, finally, to conceal the thematic serpent within as well as the serpent we expect to find *in herba*. Compared to the long sentences of Montaigne's prose, or Browne's, or Donne's, often grammatically very complex, this poetic sentence manages yet another layer of complication, since it achieves the double object of presenting a developing experience as if it were actually taking place, and of criticizing the experience's moral mode. By its syntax alone, this kind of poetic sentence presents and corrects naïveté, the while appearing spontaneous and natural. To achieve such a natural poise, the poet has had to think hard beforehand.

The second part of the poem, ten pentameter lines rhyming aabcdbcdee, manages, like the first part, to do several things at once, but quite different things and by quite different means.

> Ah, foolish Man, that would'st debase with them,
> And mortal Glory, Heavens Diadem!
> But thou who only could'st the Serpent tame,
> Either his slipp'ry knots at once untie,
> And disintangle all his winding Snare:
> Or shatter too with him my curious frame:
> And let these wither, so that he may die,
> Though set with Skill and chosen out with Care.
> That they, while Thou on both their Spoils dost tread,
> May crown thy Feet, that could not crown thy Head.

The sentence structure is clear, often even epigrammatic, more or less what Croll has christened the 'curt period'. Compared to the first part, metrically and syntactically so much more various, the second part offers a simple and moralizing message. It is not, however, without ambiguity: 'my curious Frame', for instance, certainly refers to the garland being made (or, as some have thought, the complicated poem at that moment being written), but may also refer to the poet himself, to his body. 'So that he may die' requires 'the Serpent' as its antecedent if sense is to be satisfied, but structurally makes us consider 'my curious Frame' as a possible antecedent as well. 'These' must mean the flowers, the poet's coronet-in-the-making, although no actual antecedent is given us in the grammar. 'Both their Spoils' seems to involve the coronets and serpent's achievements, again with no pure grammatical signature; 'Spoils' is a pun, forcing at least two alternative readings of the passage. The relative pronouns alone, often in Marvell's syntax elliptical or hinge-like, produce some of the twining by which the garland-idea is given even grammatical expression.

In this poem, though, the theme relies on the 'attic' notion that elegance is deceit; the maxim is, in the poem itself, both illustrated and questioned. Within the conventions of attic-naturalistic, or rambling, syntax, the poet points to his own self-deception, experienced in a mode, the pastoral, officially designed to express sincerity, honesty and truth. That the involutions of thought can be rendered also in the plainer style of the last ten lines is an example of the poet's virtuosity, of his presenting us with a grammatical 'ping' and 'pong' in which, nonetheless, the same general message is conveyed. In his involution, the poet first shows the connection between fame and interest, then between sin and salvation, and also manages to disentangle them. That disentanglement does not make for simplicity, however: the poem's garlands, whether sacred or secular, must exist in a world flawed and even upside-down; the garlands, when they are properly made and properly offered, can 'crown' only the Saviour's feet, though they were designed to replace the crown of thorns on His head. There is no simplicity in this poem: where the poet might have achieved it, he chose complexity – and this he managed although in mode and in the syntactical contrast, he *seems* to assert simplicity. The conventions of frankness are used, then, to demonstrate the impossibility, in the fallen world, of personal sincerity; the styles officially labelled 'sincere' are used to demonstrate complexity, duplicity and double-dealing. If eloquence is deceit, then here at least the converse is not true. Plain speech has its means to deceit as well as eloquence.

In other places, Marvell can illustrate, and illustrate beautifully, the more conventional literary notion that eloquence is deceit, as the nun's speech to Isabella so magnificently demonstrates in 'Upon Appleton House'. There, false logic and glozing rhetoric shamelessly conspire in thirteen stanzas of persuasion. Even in this speech, though, a sharp glance at the syntax shows how grammar pulls against imagery as well as against logic and rhetoric. The syntax itself is extremely simple: such ambiguity as exists in the nun's long aria comes from her sly way with images, not from her sentence structure. In the nun's first stanza, there is considerable handy-dandy:

'Within this holy leisure we
Live innocently as you see.
These Walls restrain the World without,
But hedge our Liberty about.'

The last line carries its double meanings; the nun means to say
that the cloister's 'liberties' are defended by the walls, although
the reader, oriented another way, quickly gathers that it is Isabella's liberties that are curtailed by these wicked walls. Later in
the poem, Fairfax's garden is turned inside out in something the
same way; but the garden (if one may say such a thing about
so extravagant a conceit) seems earnestly and actively to be
engaged in its offensive and defensive actions, as if it were in fact
doing what the nun had claimed for the cloister :

'These Bars inclose that wider Den
Of those wild Creatures, called Men.
The Cloyster outward shuts its Gates,
And, from us, locks on them the Grates.' (stanza 13)

The nuns behave oddly : they weep, not from grief but from
'Calm Pleasure', or from a needless sort of pity; they are ornamental and think in terms of ornaments – 'Our brighter Robes
and Crowns of Gold', '*Altar's Ornaments*', 'the *Angels* in a
Crown . . . the Lillies show'ring down', 'for the Clothes, The
Sea-born Amber', 'Pearls', 'Chrystal pure with Cotton warm'.
Certainly the nun's discourse is extremely sensuous; for all her
abhorrence of 'those wild Creatures, called Men', one feels the
sensuality of her imagination. Her similes are ostentatiously
'ornamental', in the pejorative sense of stylistic purists such as
Mr Winters, because she speaks in terms of adornments and
decorations – but she does so in a syntax of remarkable plainness.
Her couplets have a claim upon that epigrammatic neatness
characteristic of the plain style, although again and again her

sentences turn out to have their own enigmas, their own puzzles and tricks of compression :

> 'What need is here of Man? unless
> These as sweet Sins we should confess.'   (stanza 23)

One must think hard about what this means: that a man is needed only because a priest can hear confessions, and a priest can only be a man; but also, the nun implies that her cloister has no need for confession itself, since these are the only things they do which might be construed as confessable sins. From the syntax, 'these' appear to be the conserving of cool jellies, the preparation of sachets, occupations called 'sweet' because of the taste and odor of the things worked on; in the nun's mind, such things can be regarded as sinful only by the most puritanical standards. She banters, of course, not only with confession but with sin and virtue as well : anyone who says that such things are the worst 'sins' of which she is guilty is self-evidently guilty of self-deception, at least.

'These as sweet sins' is also an example of the literalizing of figure. By strict standards of conventual behavior, all this sweet-making for a proudly proclaimed 'Delight' and 'Pleasure' is improper; the nun's ironical tone, designed to make fun of puritanical critics of their life, turns back on her in enveloping irony shared by writer and reader. By calling a spade a spade, the poet manages to suggest that it is in fact, in the nun's mind, something quite different; again, Marvell experiments, in quite a different way from that of 'The Coronet', with the deceits possible in plain speech. By the nun's way of speaking, we are led to suspect the truth of her argument.

These games with plain speech, or with one kind of plain speech overlaid by another kind of speech far less plain, force us back to Marvell's curious ways with language. He was able to adjust language in many ways: in 'On a Drop of Dew', he mana-

T.M.P.—H

aged to 'elevate' the second half of his poem by the simple device of making the rhyme scheme more regular (a modification of Herbert's trick in 'The Altar'). In 'Clorinda and Damon', he demonstrates the agon by breaking up the lines, so that the speakers cannot speak whole couplets as they debate their positions. The poet only allows them to return to full lines when they reach agreement and find the moral solution to their problem, thus 'solving' the poem as well.

Marvell was a poet of enormous precision; his vocabulary is remarkably exact, and in his short lines, he manages to honor sense, metrics and subtlety in a way few poets in English have. By his very exactness, the limitations upon language he accepts and sets, he often points to linguistic duplicity. The trick of unmetaphoring is allied to this: Marvell directs attention at once to the absurdity and the reality of figure itself, relinquishing neither the one nor the other, insisting that readers experience anew not only the highly figurative nature of poetic language, but the figurative nature of all language. His strong sense of etymology ('fetters/feet', 'manacled/hands', *acies* as both 'glance' and 'edge') brings to a focus his concern for the manifoldness of single words: he seems to have understood the historical and psychological connotations surrounding the official denotations of any given word, and to have set himself to exploration of the problem. Though he so often rejects a conventional phrase, a conventional association, a conventional theme, he does not do so, I think, so much out of repugnance for its 'untruthfulness', as some simplifying critics would have it, as out of a desire to understand the reasons for the convention. So he redefines figures, or transfers a figure or device from its customary range to another; because he thinks so much about figures, he gives us, literally, figures of thought, figures for thinking about.

An element of Marvell's style, now much discussed in the critical literature, is his *argutia, acutezza*, sharpness of image and conceit, recently defined as a major element of the metaphysical style.[2] Obviously, one way to achieve sharpness is grammatical, in the 'curt period' of epigram, which may be either extremely clear or, though verbally extremely precise, ambiguous by reason of that conciseness. Syntactical hooking is another means of compressing two things into one, chiefly accomplished by hinge-words, or link-words; that is, by the use of a single word bearing a different relation to its dependent grammatical units. 'Nip in the blossome all our Hopes, and Thee', for instance, in 'Little T.C.', would not escape the freshman-English teacher's red pencil, sinning as it does against parallelism; Marvell's use of relative pronouns with no absolute antecedent has been referred to. The 'their' and 'these' of 'The Coronet' are cases in point; 'Whose Columnes', in the first stanza of 'Upon Appleton House', is a syntactical pivot, 'whose' referring both to 'a Model' and to the 'Forrain *Architect*', who in turn appears as both 'that' and 'who' in otherwise parallel relative clauses. In stanza 10 of that poem, the last word of the first couplet requires some search to be properly attached to its antecedents; 'Frontispiece', 'Furniture', 'House', and 'Inn' all recommend themselves.

> Him *Bishops-Hill*, or *Denton* may,
> Or *Bilbrough*, better hold then they :

this couplet is noticeably vernacular, informal, awkward, with Bilbrough as it were added late to the list. Its informality may make it seem natural, but it does not noticeably clarify meaning. 'Him' is Fairfax, or, more exactly, 'Its *Lord*', of stanza 9. Since the last line of that stanza – 'Its *Lord* a while, but not remain' – recoils to deal with the quality of the house, not of Fairfax, the 'Him' by which the next stanza must be hooked to 'Its *Lord*' is odd : the sense seems to be shifted once again in yet another direction. In stanza 62, the relative pronoun joins two different grammatical and referential elements : the heroes of the families

of Vere and Fairfax and the oaks of Appleton's wood, which
are fused into a single image :

> Of whom though many fell in War,
> Yet more to Heaven shooting are :

The first line seems to refer to soldiers, since trees do not
customarily go to war; the second plays on 'shooting' to return
to the notion of trees, which certainly are the 'they' of the next
couplet, governing both verbs.

At other times, pronouns are ambiguous : in 'An Horatian
Ode', the lines

> Did thorough his own Side
> His fiery way divide,

have never been glossed to everyone's satisfaction. Did Cromwell
like the lightning break through *himself*, or through his
group of partisans? Later, in the lines

> And *Caesars* head at last
> Did thorough his Laurels blast,

it is not altogether clear who is Caesar – the King, as monarch
in some sense a 'Caesar', whose 'head' somehow makes Cromwell's wreath imperfect; or Cromwell properly crowned by the
laurel. Still later in that poem, we come upon graver difficulties
with 'he', who becomes 'the Royal Actor', Charles I. 'He' can be
no one else :

> *He* nothing common did or mean
> Upon that memorable Scene :

but the strict antecedent is lines away. In 'An Horatian Ode' in
general, one comes up against shifts in point of view which Croll
regards as typical of a style he finally (confusingly) labelled

'baroque', and which Leo Spitzer has called 'perspectivism'. An example is this famous passage :

> Then burning through the Air he went,
> And Pallaces and Temples rent :
> And *Caesars* head at last
> Did thorough his Laurels blast
> 'Tis Madness to resist or blame
> The force of angry Heavens flame :
> And, if we would speak true,
> Much to the Man is due.

The 'he' of the first two lines is certainly Cromwell, and the 'his' of the fourth probably also; the fifth and sixth lines turn into a moral axiom, spoken in a different tone and breaking the speed of the narrative thitherto; in turn, this modulates into a pair of lines assuming great intimacy between writer and reader, thoroughly in each other's confidence. The passage moves from highly formalized and hyperbolical ritual action to extraordinary vernacular, as for the reader's private ear the poet were willing to drop his official heroics for an honest assessment of a situation obviously very difficult for both reader and writer to judge.

Indeed, much of this poem's difficulty lies in its presentation of the *situation*'s difficulties : Charles is a true king, like Richard II. Cromwell, like Bolingbroke, is a true ruler. One way in which the problematical situation is kept so problematical is by the shifts in point of view through the poem; the speaker shifts his own point of view, now speaking as if divinely appointed to characterize events, now probing them and testing them, revising his judgments on historical events, revising his rhetorical perspectives upon his subject. Perhaps the regular shift from tetrameter to trimeter encourages rapid shifts of other kinds. In the four lines

> Nor call'd the *Gods* with vulgar spight
> To vindicate his helpless Right,
> But bow'd his comely Head,
> Down as upon a Bed.

for instance, the public and political vocabulary of the first pair
of lines alters into domestic privacy; public exhortation gives way
to private prayer, as the head is 'bow'd' in ritual submission. In another place, the moralized objective description of a falcon's
typical behavior, given in a rather stiff syntax

> She, having kill'd, no more does search,
> But on the next green Bow to pearch;

changes into colloquialism as the falcon is recaptured, quite
naturally : 'The Falckner has her sure.'

One can interpret the syntactical and tonal shifts of the 'Ode'
in terms of its problematical subject; tonal shifts have many
other effects in Marvell's poetry, too. In 'The Nymph complaining', for instance, the girl's innocence is in part communicated by
the childishness of some of her sentences :

> I'me sure I never wisht them ill;
> Nor do I for all this; nor will :

> . . . nay and I know
> What he said then; I'me sure I do.

> And when 'thad left me far away,
> 'Twould stay, and run again, and stay.

> O help ! O help ! I see it faint :

> O do not run too fast. . . .

Against this naïveté are set other stylistic elements which call into
question the speaker's attitude to the Nymph's innocence, the

place of such innocence in the world, even in the sheltered world
she creates for herself. Occasionally a single word, rare in poetry
(in this case rare even in technical usage), breaks upon the
fiction of innocence to make clear how the speaker manipulates
the little nymph. 'Deodands' is such a word, clean out of the
girl's possible vocabulary. In quite another way, the sophisticat-
ed caesural variation gives away the poet's experienced detachment, so much greater than the girl's :

> Ungentle men ! They cannot thrive
> To kill thee. Thou neer didst alive
> Them any harm : alas nor cou'd
> Thy death yet do them any good.

The word order manages to suggest the girl's unpremeditated
sorrow, its twisted grammar the 'attic' result of her sincerity and
spontaneity; at the same time, the word order stresses the
exigencies of meter and rhyme, perforce altering the normal
speaking order in obedience, not to the girl's spontaneity, but to
a prior contract between the poet and his work of art. In the word
'alive' especially, rhyme manages to shift stress so that meaning is
refreshed, as also in the couplet

> There is not such another in
> The World to offer for their Sin.

The stress on the word 'in' – which makes the object of that in-
significant preposition, 'the World', so much more important
just *because* of the unimportance of 'in' – is not, I think,
accidental : ending the line on 'in', which then rhymes with the
important word 'Sin', shows the girl's naïveté in the very un-
poetical quality of the couplet. One could go on, to the substance of the couplet : the fact that so many people have read
the white fawn as a figure for Christ is an indication, it seems

to me, of their mis-reading the Nymph's utterance for the poet's.
What is sad, if sweet, about her bereavement is that she expresses
it in terms which ought to be reserved for the Saviour.

In this poem, point of view is established in very simple ways.
The nymph refers everything to herself: we start with a description of an event, the death of the little animal, which remains
unmotivated, described only by the word 'wanton'. The girl cannot and does not conceive of any reason for killing casually; it
never occurs to her to analyze either behavior or motive. Like
a child, she reacts to events as they take place, looking neither
before nor after. We must infer the troopers' motives, or habits,
as we must infer Sylvio's: their acts are inconceivable in the
nymph's world, even though they happen into that world, and
she does not attempt to consider *why* such acts take place. The
peculiarly distant narrative objectivity with which the poem begins shifts, as we read, to something else: the nymph's over-
riding effort to express her feelings. What might have gone into
analysis is all used up in merely speaking out of her tumultuous
state of mind; only her own feelings can command her attention. The first person pronoun clusters in lines 7–12, as in other
sections of the poem (e.g., lines 26–30, 44–8, 60–1), to demonstrate the innocent welling-up of her young ego. It is worth
noting that where there are several 'I's', this word is not always
metrically stressed, though it normally is:

> But I am sure, for ought that I
> Could in so short a time espie,

> I have a Garden of my own,
> But so with Roses over grown,
> And Lillies, . . .

> Among the beds of Lillyes, I
> Have sought it oft, where it should lye; . . .

> I in a golden Vial will
> Keep these two crystal Tears; and fill
> It till it do o'reflow with mine;
>
> O do not run too fast : for I
> Will but bespeak thy Grave, and dye.
>
> For I so truly thee bemoane,
> That I shall weep though I be Stone :
>
> For I would have thine Image be
> White as I can, though not as Thee.

The effect of all this is certainly to show the narrowly confined emotional vision of the nymph, myopically self-regarding; her garden and her pet, are, in the end, projections of herself and her own strongly aesthetic needs. She is as candid as her own preference for whiteness; but this endearing candor, so openly expressed, is limited by her total failure to conceive of more complicated motives than those she can identify in herself. Again, a simple rhetoric, delicately varied, points to simplistic self-concern; or, points to the fact that plain speech is no guarantee of self-understanding.

Two points of comparison immediately offer themselves : the one, Damon's speech on himself, a set-piece encased within what seems the poet's objective view of the total Damon-world; the other, the use of the first-person pronoun in 'The Garden'. In 'Damon the Mower', the first-personal words are often in stressed position :

> Tell me where I may pass the Fires . . .

> To what cool Cave shall I descend,

> I am the Mower *Damon*, known
> Through all the Meadows I have mown.
> On me the Morn her dew distills. . . .

ROSALIE L. COLIE

This Sithe of mine . . .

Yet am I richer far in Hay.

As in 'The Nymph complaining', where several first-person pronouns cluster, the pronoun here does not need always to stand in stressed position; the egocentric point is made by frequency rather than by stress. In 'The Garden', the word 'I' is never in stressed position, and occurs in only three stanzas of the nine (2, 3, 5). One result of this is, I think, to emphasize the retired literary place of this speaker. In stanza 6, the most famous stanza of the poem, 'I' does not appear; 'the Mind' is the subject of the sentence as of the stanza. In stanza 7, 'my soul', liberated from 'the Bodies Vest', is called 'it', and referred to as if the poet's personality were not identified with that soul, but rather remained in the 'vest', temporarily left on the ground. The detachments of both modes of ecstasy, then, are faithfully rendered in the language. Part of the coolness of 'The Garden' lies in this curious detachment of the speaker from 'himself', as in 'The Nymph complaining' and 'The unfortunate Lover', the coolness derives from the detachment between speaker and suffering subject.

In 'Upon Appleton House', the nun's speech, so often exploited in this book, serves to illustrate something else in Marvell's verse, the manipulations of pseudo-logic. As Croll puts it, there are many conjunctions with no logical *plus*-force, which simply reinforce a statement or idea with several examples or variants. Sometimes the elements of the argument are arranged in logical sequence, the conclusions effected by tense-indications :

'Your voice, the sweetest of the Quire,
Shall draw *Heav'n* nearer, raise us higher.
And your Example, if our Head,
Will soon us to perfection lead.

> Those Virtues to us all so dear,
> Will straight grow Sanctity when here :
> And that, once sprung, increase so fast
> Till Miracles it work at last.'   (stanza 21)

At other times, the semblance of logic is given to alogical statements by means of conjunctions : 'For', 'unless', 'Yet', 'But'. In stanza 25, the odd repetitiousness of 'but' in two entirely different grammatical uses sets the teeth on edge :

> 'But what is this to all the store
> Of Joys you see, and may make more !
> Try but a while, if you be wise :'

A more famous example is a couplet (in stanza 71) from the wood-episode in 'Upon Appleton House' :

> Or turn me but, and you shall see
> I was but an inverted Tree.

The reader's attention is caught by the solecism, but somehow not altogether displeased with it : the doubling of 'but' increases the peculiar contrary-to-factness of the fancy, operating grammatically to qualify the statement, as in quite a different range of literary language, the double-inversion ('Antipodes' etc.) in the last stanza serves to stress upside-downness and also to deny it.

The nun, of course, uses pseudo-logical conjunctions to weave her fragile dialectic into a net to catch the coney Isobel : a semblance of, or substitute for, logical construction recurs throughout Marvell's poetry, in many places where deception is not the aim. 'The Definition of Love' has 'And yet', 'For', 'And therefore', 'Unless', 'As', 'But' and 'Therefore'; 'To His Coy Mistress', 'Had we', 'We would', 'For', 'But', 'Now therefore' and 'Thus'. In 'The Garden', the careful progression of points is not marked by such signals of logic;[3] the method of hiatus in that poem leaps over official connective and conjunction, to permit us only at the end to see how 'logically', or anthologically, a series of tableaux, exemplifying alternative modes of perception, has been offered us, in strict progression of the soul's ascent and return. In 'Upon Appleton House', the pseudo-logical conjunctions – especially 'but' (st. 3, 4, 10, 29, 32, 33, 34, 36, 40, 41, 43, 44, 45, 46, 47, 48, 51, 61, 65, 66, 68, 69, 70, 71, 78, 82, 86, 88, 89, 90, 91, 95, 96, 97), 'For', 'Yet', 'Therefore', 'So' and 'Thus' – are sprinkled across the poem, making another connective net to hold together its thrashing elements.

That the conjunctions express connections made on the basis of perception and emotion, rather than on the basis of logic, is really irrelevant, is an example of Marvell's peculiar translation of ideas and philosophical structures into purely poetical terms. If anything, this 'false' net of connectives is another pointer to the instability and disruption stressed throughout the poem; here, logical expectations remain unfulfilled, although the pseudo-logical words have a connective value of their own. Translation of the expressive language of one discipline – in this case, logic – into the language of poetry is consistent with Marvell's general attitude of experimentation; in the case of 'Upon Appleton House', this pseudo-logical linguistic experiment is parallel to many different kinds of experiment and expression of problematics. In this particular case, logic was simply one conventional range of expression which he distorted from its traditional function to serve poetic purposes of his own.

One of Marvell's characteristic habits was to shift the grammatical position of a word so that one sentence or one line must be read in two quite different ways; his sleight-of-hand with relative pronouns is one conspicious example of this maneuver. ' 'Tis not, what once it was, the World' presents a problem of paraphrase, so does, in 'Upon Appleton House',

> Dark all without it knits; within
> It opens passable and thin; (stanza 64)

What part of speech is 'without'? And, related to that, the first 'it'? In both cases, the wood turns out to be 'it' – that is, the wood knits, and the wood opens; but 'Dark' too makes its claim to be taken, for a moment at least, as the subject, not the object, of 'knits'. 'Dark all without', furthermore, seems to be parallel to 'the Night within' of the preceding line (at the end of the preceding stanza), so that one expects a guide from stanza to stanza which in fact turns out not to exist. The grammatical trick effects not a connective but a reversal; we discover that the 'Night within' will become the light of the wood's 'passable and thin' interior. Sometimes grammatical ambiguities are not important : it would be foolish to argue for deep significance in each and every syntactical oddity in Marvell's verse, some of which must be the result of simple carelessness on the poet's part, or the proofreader's, or of the state of the manuscript posthumously published. Furthermore, the images of the former world as chaos and of the wood are clear, even if the syntax is not. Nor does it much matter whether the poet speaks of three different flowers or of two different colors in the line 'That of the Tulip Pinke and Rose'; with or without commas, the line makes sense.

'Nip in the blossome all our hopes and Thee' plays with degrees of metaphor as well as with 'nip' as a syntactical pivot : the line begins as a cliché, and gains power as we realize that T.C. is taken, throughout the poem, as a 'flower', and that both girl and flowers are symbols of transience. A simpler example of a grammatical pivot is the line in 'Tom May's Death', 'By this *May* to himself and them was come', another striking failure of parallelism which allows a rather doggerel wit, fitting the kind of inferior accomplishment Marvell attributes to May. Such grammatical pivots are often in effect puns : 'sound' in 'And not of one of the bottom sound', from 'Mourning'. In the line 'Since this ill Spirit is possest', of the 'Dialogue', there are several double meanings (ill, Spirit, possest) to make this one of the most notionally complicated lines of all Marvell's verse. 'It' is either the subject or the object of 'possest'; by either reading, the line makes sense.

Marvell's puns are difficult to avoid discussing. Sometimes a grammatical pivot is indistinguishable from a pun; sometimes a quibble focuses several meanings in a single word – and, in 'The Garden', a series of puns seems to keep alive a consistent series of different meanings, sometimes the poet 'unpuns', as he unfigures and unmetaphors. Frequently there is a late resonance to his double meanings : their implications follow at some distance from the words themselves. 'Fly from their Ruine', in 'Upon Appleton House', stanza 28, is such a phrase : the nun's plan would 'ruin' Isabella; the nunnery ultimately becomes a 'ruin' on the estate. *'Virgin Buildings oft brought forth'* seems to make a figure about the provenance of the new Appleton House from the stones of the old; only later do we realize that Marvell was getting his licks in at the Roman Church. Still later, we realize the thematic connection between this remark, about the Cistercian nunnery, and the swelling house honoring its master and designer. 'A Dialogue between the Soul and Body' plays on 'possest'; 'Upon Appleton House' plays on 'dispossest'. 'Dispensed' is a quibble, as is 'imbark' – and so on, and on. Sometimes a pun echoes another denotation, as in the questionable 'quaint' of 'To his Coy Mistress' or 'The Scales of either Eye' in 'Eyes and Tears'. Occasionally Marvell may have made a mistake, so to speak, suggesting a double meaning not actually present, as in the word 'scale' in the line 'And Fishes do the Stables scale', from 'Upon Appleton House'.

Sometimes a play on a word extends a figure, or a common locution, as in stanza 40 of 'Upon Appleton House', where the 'guard stars' around the North Star are called 'the vigilant *Patroul* / Of Stars [that] walks round about the Pole'; or in 'Eyes and Tears', where the word 'captivating' leads the poet to his figure of the Magdalene's tears as 'liquid Chaines'. These chains 'fetter her Redeemers feet' – that is, they captivate, or make captive. In 'A Dialogue between the Soul and Body', the fetters-feet, manacled-hands plays extend the notion in 'Eyes and Tears', exploring etymology to end in unpunning. The metaphorical meanings are collapsed back into their literal origin: so Damon 'discovers' the meadows as he strips them of their protective grass, or the nun's tongue 'suckt' Isabella in. In the 'Horatian Ode', the sense of *pictus*, painted, in 'Pict' may have suggested the word 'party-colour'd' for Scots. Because of their tartans, of course, and their outspoken political partisanship, 'party-colour'd' is an apt pun even without the notion of 'pictus'. The tortoises are encased 'In cases fit of Tortoise shell': that is, of their natural condition, a metaphor seems to be made, although in fact the poet tautologically describes their shells. Nonetheless, because of his wording, which applies to the artificial cases for other things made of tortoiseshell, he succeeds in confounding for a moment the natural with the artifical world. By these means, the process of metaphor is exposed to the reader's examination; we see how metaphors are made.

There are anomalies in this practice, too, as I need hardly say – the poet who can do so many different things, can so maneuver styles of diction, syntax, and imagery, who can so manipulate persona and tone, obviously chooses to be associated or connected with no one style, no one school of verse. A reader might be forgiven for assuming that Marvell donned and doffed styles as if they were garments hanging ready for him; for assuming, perhaps, with a school of modern American stylistic critics distinguished for their own stylishness, that all there is to Marvell's verse is its capacity to assume styles. For such critics, the style of a literary work – its language, its tone – is its whole substance. 'Style' is simply – or complexly – a shimmering screen on which an illusory reality is made to appear, is, indeed, the only reality attributable to a work of art. Certainly in a crude sense, this is always so – in a literary work, all we have is words, those chosen and those not chosen, separated by intervals of silence, by intervals of space. There was no Anna Karenina, no Hamlet; still less was there a Nymph or Maria, as the poet conceives her in his poem. Art *is* illusion. But some illusions are more illusory than others; or some illusions direct us at once to considerations of reality (Rembrandt, Goya, Cézanne) even when they are 'about' illusion, inevitably constructed of materials and conventions having nothing specific to do with the 'reality' to which the painters seem to point.[4] We know what 'betrayal' means from Rembrandt's 'Saint Peter' in the Rijksmuseum although the trick with the maidservant's candle is technically *chic* beyond measure – the technical trick does not detract from but rather manages to enhance the moral meaning of the painting. We know what gratuitous violence 'means' from Goya's pictures of the French wars, what rocks are, in all their hardness, from Cézanne's extremely stylized geology. In Marvell's 'style', both the precision of some of his images – the Nymph's garden, say, or the emblematic environment of the unfortunate Lover – and the diaphanousness of others (in particular, the middle stanzas of 'The Garden') relate to a context of ideas, even of morality, to which they unmistakably direct the reader. The 'concreteness' of these ideas and impressions, the concreteness, then, of the most elusive elements of our life, forces us through sensory perception to intellectual perception. We are set to think about the range, even about the decorum, within the conscious concept of style; we are asked to consider the reasons for style, and for choosing any particular aspect of style over any other. Even at the level of individual words –

'Deodands', 'Corslet', 'green' – Marvell acts as critic of his poetic materials, reexamining the elements which make up style and asking us, as critical readers, to examine them too. The poet-as-critic forces the job of criticism upon his readers, involves his readers inextricably in his own professional problems.

S O U R C E : *'My Ecchoing Song' – Andrew Marvell's Poetry of Criticism* (1970).

NOTES

1. Yvor Winters, 'The Sixteenth Century Lyric in England', *Poetry*, LII-LIV (1939); Wesley Trimpi, *Ben Jonson's Poems. A Study of the Plain Style* (Stanford, 1962); Douglas L. Peterson, *The English Lyric from Wyatt to Donne* (Princeton, 1967).

2. For some discussion of this, see J. A. Mazzeo, *Renaissance and Seventeenth Century Studies* (New York, 1964) pp. 29–59.

3. See J. V. Cunningham, *Tradition and Poetic Structure* (Denver, 1960) pp. 40–58.

4. Sigurd Burckhardt, 'The Poet as Fool and Priest', *English Literary History*, XXIII (1956) pp. 279–98.

SELECT BIBLIOGRAPHY

This bibliography does not include works represented in Part Three.

GENERAL

Douglas Bush, *English Literature in the Earlier Seventeenth Century: 1600–1660* (Oxford, 1945; 2nd edn, 1962).

Rosemary Freeman, *English Emblem Books* (London, 1948).

William R. Keast (ed.), *Seventeenth Century English Poetry: Modern Essays in Criticism* (New York, 1962).

Frank Kermode, 'The Dissociation of Sensibility', in *Kenyon Review*, XIX (1957).

Louis Martz, *The Poetry of Meditation* (New Haven, 1954).

Joseph A. Mazzeo, *Renaissance and Seventeenth Century Studies* (New York and London, 1964).

Marjorie Nicolson, *Science and Imagination* (New York, 1956).

D. J. Palmer and Malcolm Bradbury (eds), *Metaphysical Poetry* (London, 1969).

Mario Praz, *Studies in Seventeenth-Century Imagery* (London, 1939–47).

Ruth Wallerstein, *Studies in Seventeenth-Century Poetic* (Madison, Wisconsin, 1950).

F. J. Warnke, *European Metaphysical Poetry* (New Haven, 1961).

F. P. Wilson, *Elizabethan and Jacobean* (Oxford, 1945).

THOMAS CAREW

Rhodes Dunlap (ed.), *The Poems of Thomas Carew* (Oxford, 1957).

Edward I. Selig, *The Flourishing Wreath. A Study of Thomas Carew's Poetry* (New Haven, 1948).

JOHN CLEVELAND

H. Levin, 'John Cleveland and the Conceit', in *The Criterion*, XIV (1934–5).

Brian Morris and Eleanor Withington (eds), *The Poems of John Cleveland* (Oxford, 1967).

ABRAHAM COWLEY

R. B. Hinman, *Abraham Cowley's World of Order* (Cambridge, Mass., 1960).

A. R. Waller (ed.), *The English Writings of Abraham Cowley*, 2 vols (Cambridge, 1905–6).

RICHARD CRASHAW

L. C. Martin (ed.), *The Poems of Richard Crashaw* (Oxford, 1927; rev. 1957).

Ruth Wallerstein, *Richard Crashaw* (Madison, Wisconsin, 1935).

Austin Warren, *Richard Crashaw: A Study in Baroque Sensibility* (Baton Rouge, 1939).

G. W. Williams, *Image and Symbol in the Sacred Poetry of Richard Crashaw* (Columbia, South Carolina, 1963).

JOHN DONNE

Helen Gardner (ed.), *John Donne: The Divine Poems* (Oxford, 1952).

Helen Gardner (ed.), *John Donne: The Elegies and the Songs and Sonnets* (Oxford, 1965).

H. J. C. Grierson (ed.), *The Poems of John Donne*, 2 vols (Oxford, 1912).

Julian Lovelock (ed.), *Donne: Songs and Sonets* (London, 1973).

Arnold Stein, *John Donne's Lyrics* (Minneapolis, 1962).

Leonard Unger, *Donne's Poetry and Modern Criticism* (Chicago, 1950).

George Williamson, *The Donne Tradition* (Cambridge, Mass., 1930).

GEORGE HERBERT

F. E. Hutchinson (ed.), *The Works of George Herbert* (Oxford, 1941; rev. 1945).

L. C. Knights, 'George Herbert', in *Explorations* (London, 1946).

Arnold Stein, *George Herbert's Lyrics* (Baltimore, 1968).

Rosemond Tuve, *A Reading of George Herbert* (Chicago and London, 1952).

ANDREW MARVELL

T. S. Eliot, 'Andrew Marvell', in *Selected Essays* (New York and London, 1932).

J. B. Leishman, *The Art of Marvell's Poetry* (London, 1966).

William A. McQueen and Kiffin A. Rockwell (eds), *The Latin Poetry of Andrew Marvell* (Chapel Hill, 1964).

H. M. Margoliouth (ed.), *The Poems and Letters of Andrew Marvell* 2 vols (Oxford, 1927; rev. 1952).

Harold E. Toliver, *Marvell's Ironic Vision* (New Haven, 1965).

HENRY VAUGHAN

L. C. Martin (ed.), *The Works of Henry Vaughan* (Oxford, 1914; rev. 1957).

Louis Martz, *The Paradise Within* (New Haven, 1964).

E. C. Pettet, *Of Paradise and Light* (Cambridge, 1960).

NOTES ON CONTRIBUTORS TO
PART THREE

S. L. Bethell was Senior Lecturer in English at the University of Wales at Cardiff from 1937 until his death in 1954. His publications include *The Winter's Tale: A Study* (1947) and *The Cultural Revolution of the Seventeenth Century* (1951). His essay in this Casebook marked the beginning of a study of the theory and practise of the conceit in continental poetry, a study he never lived to complete.

Rosalie Colie (1925-75) was Professor of English, University of Toronto. Her publications include *Paradoxia Epidemica: The Renaissance Tradition of Paradox.* (1966) and *'My Ecchoing Song': Marvell's Poetry of Criticism* (1970).

Josephine Miles is Professor of English at the University of California, Berkeley, and a pioneer in the study of the language of poetry. Her publications include *The Continuity of Poetic Language* (1951) and *Eras and Modes in English Poetry* (1957). Her own poems have been published in several volumes since 1960.

Earl Miner is Professor (since 1972) of English and Comparative Literature, Princeton University. His publications include *An Introduction to Japanese Court Poetry* (1968), *Dryden's Poetry* (1967) and *The Cavalier Mode from Jonson to Cotton* (1971).

HANAN SELVIN is Professor of Sociology at the University of Rochester. His publications include *The Effects of Leadership* (1960).

LEO SPITZER, who died in 1960, taught at Johns Hopkins University from 1936 until his death. His many books and articles include studies of German, Spanish, French and Italian literature. His major English works are *Linguistics and Literary History: Essays in Stylistics* (1948) and *A Method of Interpreting Literature* (1949).

J. H. SUMMERS is Professor of English at Michigan State University. His publications include *The Muse's Method: An Introduction to Paradise Lost* (1962) and *The Lyric and Dramatic Milton* (1964).

ROSEMUND TUVE, who died in 1964, was Professor of English at the University of Pennsylvania. Her publications include *A Reading of George Herbert* (1952) and *Images and Themes in Five Poems by Milton* (1957). A selection of her previously uncollected essays, on Spenser, Herbert and Milton, appeared in 1970, edited by Thomas P. Roche Jr.

INDEX

Figures in italic denote essays or extracts in Part Three.